MW00681053

Letters to Sparky

A MEMOIR OF WORLD WAR II

Carmen Leigh Hiner
and Harold Lyle Hiner

EAKIN PRESS Austin, Texas

This book is dedicated to my husband Harold,
my brothers Richard and Henry Leigh,
and all the young men of their generation
who served their country
with honor, courage, and integrity.

For CIP
information,
please access:
www.loc.gov

FIRST EDITION
Copyright © 2002
By Carmen Leigh Hiner and Harold Lyle Hiner
Published in the United States of America
By Eakin Press
A Division of Sunbelt Media, Inc.
P.O. Drawer 90159 ☐ Austin, Texas 78709-0159
email: eakinpub@sig.net
☐ website: www.eakinpress.com ☐
ALL RIGHTS RESERVED.
1   2   3   4   5   6   7   8   9
1-57168-645-2 PB
1-57168-646-0 HB

Contents

Navy artists find strength and character in faces of heroes like Major H. L. Hiner, who was awarded the Navy Cross for bravery. Sketch depicts him when he was a second lieutenant.

Foreword

For almost fifty years, we observed our parents' love and absolute trust in each other. They shared total respect, open affection, laughter, and tears with a certain knowledge that they could always count on each other. As parents, though they enforced strict rules and required honesty and integrity, they told us often that they were proud of us and proved their unconditional love. They had confidence in our character and our hearts.

They experienced great joy and success, but they had more than their share of tragedy as well. At those times, they displayed tenderness, forgiveness, and amazing strength. During the good times, they always expressed their gratitude for our blessings: our health, happiness, love, and the strength of our family bonds. They told us that we should never take these for granted. During the heartbreaking times, we were thankful for every joyous memory and confident that we had not missed opportunities to express our love for and pride in each other.

This recognition that time spent with friends and family was invaluable and that the beauty of the world should be savored was a constant in our lives. We feel that this consciousness was born during the war years. Our father faced the prospect of death and witnessed the destruction of so many young lives. We know that he felt himself a lucky man, because he expressed his gratitude so often. Our mother suffered the war's effects here at home, worrying about her brothers, cousins, friends, and the young man who was to become our father. These two young people from small towns experienced the world in a way they never would have, had there been no war.

Watching them face these extreme challenges, illuminated through their letters, provided a clear view into their spirits. Because circumstances kept them apart and forced them to create their relationship in their writing, they revealed more of themselves than they might have otherwise. Conversation is often not as thoughtful as correspondence. Their courtship, which started with mutual attraction and common experience, carried them all over the world through the most extreme events. And through it all, they were revealing their hopes, realizations, passions, and characters.

When our father died, our mother was able to relive that communion of spirit through his letters. When she reread them, she realized that he had never complained about the time spent away from his loved ones and never felt that he was being asked to do more than his share. With this book, she wants to share the courage and commitment of this young man she was to marry with all of us. The details of their personal journeys entwined with their love story are their own, but represent the experiences and feelings of many young men and women during that war.

We have always known that we are the children of brave and honorable parents. This book allows us to glimpse who they were and what they went through together before we knew them. Our generation never had to face the sacrifices of theirs. They suffered huge losses, but the confidence and maturity that these young people gained affected the rest of their lives and changed the world that we live in.

We are so proud of our mother and honored she is willing to share this book with us. It has been a labor of love and a testament to our amazing father. We know that he would be as proud of this accomplishment as he always was of her throughout their wonderful marriage.

—CHRISTINE HINER KASTEN
and RICHARD L. HINER

Acknowledgments

When my beloved husband, Harold Lyle Hiner, died in 1996, I experienced such loneliness I felt it would be impossible to continue without him. One Sunday, I came home from church and, in desperation, brought out the packets of letters I had not read since he returned from overseas in February 1946. I intended to read a few every day. Once started, I couldn't put them down until I had read all ninety-seven of them. When I finished, I felt better than I had for a long time. Their counterpart, my letters, had been destroyed, because men in combat could not be so encumbered. His told a story and reminded me of things I had forgotten until now.

I knew then that telling the story of that six-year period was a necessity. I wanted my children and grandchildren to know all about the young man in that story. I thank them because they encouraged me to write it all down and convinced me it was an act of love. I know had it not been for them, I probably would not have done so.

I wish also to acknowledge the six other members of my writers' lab, The Writers of the Purple Page. Without their superior knowledge and training in the art of writing, their invaluable editing and their loving support, I would never have had the incentive to continue.

Vincent Langelo, a shipmate of Harold's and a man I have never met, learned of my project and encouraged me to try to publish. He has helped me along the way with advice and step-by-step information. He did this at a very busy time in his life as he just published his own book, *With All Our Might: The WWII History of the USS* Boise.

As for the picture credits, I'm grateful to the following:

Special Collections and Archives, Merrill Library at Utah State University in Logan, Utah, for the use of the photograph of a "Ski Class on Old Main Hill";

Wilmer Everly, Chief Photographer's Mate, Coast Guard, for the picture of a baptism in the sea prior to the Iwo Jima invasion;

Sergeant L. R. Burmeister, Marine Corps, for the picture of the Catholic mass on Suribachi's summit;

Press Association for the map of Iwo Jima;

Paul Queenan, Photographer's Mate Second Class, Coast Guard, for the pictures of the Fourth Marine Division's capture of the first airstrip on Iwo Jima and the Fifth Marine Division as they cleared the Japanese-held volcano and unloaded supplies on the beach;

U.S. Navy for the pictures of the U.S.S. *Boise* in action during the second battle of the Savo Sea in the Pacific, firing at tanks on the beach and recovering aircraft in the Mediterranean combat near Gela, Sicily;

Donald F. Byers, a shipmate of Harold's, for the picture of Harold with Boise officers and WAVES at the Philadelphia preview of *The Navy Comes Through* in December 1942.

Preface

Letters to Sparky is an old-fashioned love story of the World War II era, told by the two people involved. It unfolds through the ninety-seven letters a young marine wrote to a girl he dated in college, and the girl's diary, which tells what it was like for the young women whose brothers, sweethearts, and husbands went to war. The combat history is told in the omniscient voice, based on magazines, books, and news articles of that time.

Never before or since World War II has our country been so united. Young men volunteered in droves, some lying about their ages. Women joined the armed forces and replaced men in jobs left vacant by the draft. Men past draft age worked long hours to compensate for the loss of manpower, and everyone willingly supported rationing of gas, sugar, shoes, and other necessities.

It was a sad time of death, injury, and pain, but also of great heroism and sacrifice. A time that challenged every American man, woman, and child to dedicate themselves to a greater cause. Above all else, that war instilled in those who lived through it an appreciation for loved ones, for home and family, and for the privilege of living in peace.

The young marine in the story, a holder of the Navy Cross, believed that every man who showed up for that war was a hero. Greatest of all were those who died in the mud, storming beaches, in the air, or at sea, where no one around lived to tell about their acts of heroism.

The President of the United States takes pleasure in presenting the NAVY CROSS to

SECOND LIEUTENANT HAROLD L. HINER, U.S.M.C.,

for service as set forth in the following

CITATION:

"For extraordinary heroism as Number Three Turret Officer aboard the U.S.S. BOISE, during action against enemy Japanese naval forces off Cape Esperance, Guadalcanal, Solomon Islands on the night of October 11-12, 1942. Remaining at his post until his turret was put out of action by a hit on the face plate and the flooding of his handling room, Second Lieutenant Hiner, with utter disregard for his own personal safety, ordered his men out to safety while he stayed behind to perform valuable service by relaying orders from the damaged turret to Control and Central. His courageous initiative and conscientious devotion to duty were in keeping with the highest traditions of the United States Naval Service."

For the President,

James Forrestal

Acting
Secretary of the Navy.

CHAPTER 1

We Meet

Dear Diary,

Well, here I go! My last two years of college and away from home for the first time in my life! Thank heavens for speech scholarships; Butch Kimball got one, too. We were steadies our two years at B.A.C. Someday we might get married, but we've agreed for now to be friends, play the field, and have fun.

Lucille Macfarlane and I board in the home of a family right off campus. We share a room and bath (breakfast and dinner are included). She's a barrel of fun, talented in dance and music and a real beauty, except so flat-chested she thinks she looks horrible in formals. (I suggested she get a bra with a larger cup and pad it with Kleenex.)

We were being rushed by *all five houses* on campus! The Alpha Chi Omegas arranged dates for us with a couple of big shots. Truth is, we had already decided on Chi Omega. It's worthwhile, though, because Lucille's date was Vern Crockett, and they really hit it off (maybe the Kleenex helped). My date, Roland Reading, is tall, good-looking and captain of the basketball team. He's nice ... we had fun, but we're not each other's type. He's a jock and I'll bet he has a steady. Besides, he's prettier than I am and I'm smarter than he is.

I'm really excited about my major. According to the catalog it's Commerce, not Political Science. I like the head of the department, Professor Milt Merrill, who is my advisor. Butch and I are on the varsity debate team ... we'll probably be partners.

———— 🦃 ————

I really like Logan, Utah. It's a great college town, not too big. The campus is beautiful ... crawling with lots of really good-looking guys ... *Oooh la laaaa*! I like to watch the ROTC guys drill in the quadrangle during lunch hour. I'd love to be one of the girl sponsors and march with them, dressed in a spiffy uniform. But sponsors are chosen their freshman year, so entering as a junior is too late for that.

I'm glad I pledged Chi Omega. I've met some really nifty girls ... Alice Randall, Willy Wilcox, Marge Hanson, the Wintch sisters, and my big sister from Ogden, June Coop. She has her own car ... *lucky me*. Bob Elkins is our houseboy. We call him Sister Bob. He knows just about everybody so is a good source of information about the other guys on campus. This last weekend the Chi Omegas had a picnic in the park, and that's where I saw the best-looking guy I've ever seen in my WHOLE life! I hope he's a student ... wish I knew his name so I could ask Sister Bob about him. I was walking down a path to the restroom and he was walking toward me. The sun was filtering through the tall trees, shining on his blonde hair (I say I prefer brunettes, but I always fall for blondes). He's tall, with the build of a Greek god (if Hitler saw him, he'd kidnap him to help create the pure Aryan race he's so paranoid about). He smiled at me and said "Hello!" I almost fainted; I would have willingly followed him to wherever he was going, but didn't want to appear too forward. I had a funny, tingling feeling and wondered where I had seen or known him before. I haven't been able to figure it out ... maybe in another life?

———— 🦃 ————

I saw that great-looking blonde guy again. Yes, he's a student. I wish I knew his name. I was walking up the hill to Old Main for my eight o'clock, hurrying because I was running late. There he was in front of me! His ankle was in a cast, he was on crutches, a briefcase under one arm. The walk was icy and it was slow going for him. I caught up to him, intending to ask if I could carry his briefcase for him, but didn't have the nerve, he looked so embarrassed. He mumbled something about a skiing accident.

I should have insisted. Why do I get tongue-tied when I'm around this guy? My family calls me "Motor-Mouth." They'd never believe I was *ever* at a loss for words.

Jack Caine asked me to the Military Ball, and there *he* was. At intermission the ROTC did a "Silent Drill." I've never seen that done. It's fantastic ... totally impressive! *He* led the drill ... Jack told me he's Regimental Adjutant. Wouldn't you know, in all that big ballroom, we're standing right behind *his* date. I heard her comments about him, and all I could think was, What's he doing with that tacky girl? Still don't know his name.

Finally, I know *his* name ... Harold Hiner. The student-body elections have been going on, and the Sigma Nus and Foresters ran him for president, and he won. The Sigma Chis and Pi Kaps are still in shock.

The night after the election, I went to the Varsity Show with Conway Sonne, and who are we sitting behind? The new student-body president-elect and that GIRL! *What does he see in her?*

Well, things are looking up ... I've met Harold Hiner. In yesterday's assembly, the Alpha Sigma Nu honorary members were announced. To my surprise, I made it. Six men and six women, presumably "distinguished for activity, personality, and scholarship." Not to my surprise, *he* made it, and so did Butch. A meeting followed the assembly, and *he* was the only one I hadn't already met. He introduced himself and said, "I've been wishing I knew your name. I think freckles are darn cute."

The Chi Omegas are responsible for the last assembly of the year. We've arranged for a swell vocal and instrumental group from BYU, whose soloist plays a rip-roarin' guitar and is an outstanding yodeler. It's a variety show around the theme of a travelogue.

When I told my mother and Aunt Alt I was planning Chairman and M.C., they sent me a dress they thought I would love. I do ... it's a white crepe sheath with two-inch rows of fringe from the shoulder seams to the bottom of the long skirt. When the *body* moves, the fringe does likewise, and it "emphasizes the positive." *Perfect!* Just what I need for the assembly.

From the stage, I could see Harold in the front row, grinning from ear to ear, obviously impressed with the entertainment. As the curtain closed on the rousing finale, he dashed up the back stairs to the stage and congratulated everyone, looked at me, and said, "Sparky, that was sensational ... and so were you ... may I call you?"

So, he did call, and we've had some dates. I don't know if he's still seeing *that girl,* but next year will be his second senior year. He could graduate this year and get a Marine Corps commission under the Morrill Act. He works summers and holidays like the rest of us, and has put himself through college. He decided to take a fifth year (thank goodness), take some classes he's been wanting but couldn't fit into his forestry schedule, and have some fun.

I can relate to that. Everyone with any sense knows this country is going to be in a war soon. It's just a matter of time until even the isolationists wake up and realize two oceans are not a safety net.

He'll be president of the student-body next year, so he might as well make the most of it. It's obvious I'm not the only girl on campus who thinks he's a dreamboat ... he's also a swell guy and has nice manners. I like that.

UTAH STATE UNIVERSITY 1940–41

It's good to be back in school, though I hate to think about this being my last year. Living in the Chi Omega house is swell.

I love the curved staircase to the main floor. Every time I go down it during the day, I practice so when I have a date waiting in the entryway at the foot of the stairs, I can make a grand entrance ... float down, if I have on a frothy dress—or slink down, if I'm being worldly. If I'm wearing a formal, I lift the skirt a bit so I won't stumble (it doesn't hurt to show a little leg). If my date is looking up at me with a smile on his face, I know it's going to be a fun date. The house mother's room is right next to the front entrance so she'll know if we come in on time. Sister Bob is still with us, a good friend and source of all knowledge in the dating world. From him I learned that Harold and *that girl* broke up for good during the summer. Whoopeeee! Praise the Lord, and pass the ammunition!

There's a different feeling in the air this fall. It's partly the realization that soon we'll be going out into the real world, but mostly a foreboding about the future. For me, it's what will I do when I leave this safe environment I've loved? I've thought about that a lot these past two years. I know what I want to do ... go to law school and then into politics. Of course, I'm a romantic and want to get married and have children ... when the right one comes along. How will all this fit into what I think is ahead?

When I was home this summer I visited with Congressman Walter Granger. My mother campaigns her heart out whenever he's up for reelection. She even named my brother for him. He knows what I want to do and has told my parents if I need money, he will loan it to me. It never occurred to me I couldn't do anything I wanted to do.

Then I talked to Dr. Merrill. I expected him to be pleased, but he's discouraging me. He says the chances of a woman getting into law school are slim unless she comes from a family of judges or lawyers in established firms. He agrees my grades are good enough and knows I can speak and think on my feet. I'm the only senior girl in Political Science and rank second in the department ... Butch is first. I trust Dr. Merrill's judgment and I know he likes me; still he believes, if I have to borrow money, it would be a mistake. I'll admit I cried for days when I could be alone (usually in the bathroom). I guess I have to be sensible and consider alternatives ... get a teacher's certificate just in case. Why is it most men seem to think women shouldn't want a career except as a nurse, teacher, or secretary? My dad and my brothers don't feel that way.

The dating scene is great! The really big events are coming up, like the Military Ball, Foresters' Ball, Varsity Show, and fraternity and sorority formals. In addition to SMOOTH Mel Manning, I've been dating Jack Caine, Keith Sorenson, and Jack's cousin, Eccles Caine ... kind of funny, but can't resist a guy who calls me "Charmin' Carmen" and picks me up after my last class in his dad's car. He's fun, has a goofy sense of humor, and is willing to be just a friend.

Harold asks me out quite a bit, but having just got out of a serious relationship, he's doing what he said he was going to do—making up for lost time and having fun. He's dating at least one girl in every sorority house, I think! The other night we had a date and Imogene Lee came upstairs and announced, "Harold Hiner's downstairs, but I don't know whose beau he is." He's a BMOC, so what would you expect. HOPE HE ISN'T FALLING IN LOVE!

There is an undercurrent of urgency in the attitude of the guys and girls, especially the seniors. All you hear these days is, Who's getting pinned? I can understand why couples who have been steadies since high school would be planning to marry when they graduate, but why someone on a first or second date wants to get serious and committed throws me.

Is it the prospect of war, I wonder? The need to know there is someone for you, even if you don't really know each other very well? This year I've been out with guys I've known as friends for a long time and now, all of a sudden, they want to get to third base and set the date all in one night. I talked to Dean Lenore

Williams, and asked her what she thought. She said, "It's the primal urge of men going to war who want to make sure their seed is sown." I know what seed she's talking about, but I had to look up the word "primal" in the dictionary. I guess it makes sense. Some girls I know are just as frantic. I cringe when I hear a girl say, "You know if you're married you get an allotment."

My teacher's training is at West Logan High School, and I love it! Miss Johnson has turned the debating team over to me ... I'm their coach. I guess I'm a good teacher, but I do feel sad that I can't go to law school. Am I a quitter to give up without more of a struggle? I've been interviewed by high school principals around the state and have several offers, including West Logan. Cedar City is building a brand-new high school. I've decided to sign a contract with Principal Barlow and go home for a year. It will be good for my parents. My brother Ham is already in California with the National Guard and brother Dick is thinking of joining the Air Force even though he's married. At the end of that time I may have a better idea as to what I want to do.

I'm dating Harold quite a bit now. The same offer he had last year of a regular commission in the Marine Corps has been renewed. I hate to think about it, but every guy graduating, regardless of his major, knows he's going into the service. Even Butch, who hasn't been in ROTC and has vision problems, wants to join the navy.

Harold invited me to the Foresters' Ball and the Sigma Nu spring picnic. At the picnic, he asked me to their spring formal. He's going to hitchhike home to Pocatello, Idaho, and drive back in his folks' car so we can go in style. I'm so excited! I've decided to invite him to the Chi O spring formal. He says I'm the only girl he's been with lately who can keep up with him on a hike. These long, skinny legs are good for something, I guess.

————🎺————

The Sigma Nu formal was peachy keen! My corsage was pink camellias, a nice change from gardenias that get brown at the slightest touch ... or hug. First there was a banquet at the Blue Bird Cafe. Harold was M.C., and was he great! The favors, little gold evening bags, are darling, and we danced to the smooth music of Eldy Hansen's orchestra. I love it when they turn the lights low and you can dance close to a slow, romantic melody like "In the Mood," or "Sentimental Journey" ... especially when you like the guy you're with.

Best of all was the privacy of being in a car with just each other. It was like being in our own little, cozy world. We had a chance to kiss and cuddle and the luxury of talking seriously about our feelings ... and fears. Can you imagine ... we both played second-chair violin in orchestra! Why is it I find myself comparing other dates to him and find them lacking? It's obvious I'm only one of many on his list, but still I really believe he likes me.

When we got back to the Chi O house, we sat for a while, not wanting the evening to end. I'll never forget as long as I live what he said then.

"I really care about you, Sparky. I've been wanting to tell you how I feel about my immediate future. I planned to go into the Forest Service, but instead will be reporting for duty in the Marine Corps, September 2nd. With that duty you are hardly ever stateside, especially in wartime. I know the kinds of things I'll be called upon to do. I couldn't do a good job and worry about a wife at home. When I marry, I want to be *with* my wife. I don't worry so much about being killed as being crippled or maimed. I couldn't face coming home as less than a man and being a burden to a woman I loved. It's not fair to ask someone to wait with the uncertainty I'm facing." (He drew me closer.) "I want you to know I think you are special! Will you write to me? I promise I'll write as often as I can, and hopefully this war will not be a long one." We kissed!!

I didn't doubt the sincerity of his words, and they made sense ... I guess. I really can't see being married and having your husband gone to God knows where. The same feeling came over me as did the first time I saw him ... Where have I known this person before? Only this time, I wondered how I could stand it if anything bad happened to him.

"Yes, I will write ... I think you're special, too." I wanted to say more, but I was too shy. This wasn't the time.

Ski class on Old Main Hill, 1940.

Harold, Carmen, and Butch, "Buzzer" yearbook photos as Alpha Sigma Nu Honorees, 1941.

HAROLD HINER: Dislikes Engineers but is fond of Foresters, hunting and shooting, thick steaks, walking, reading, rain and military ... student body president ... rifle squad ... Blue Key ... Sigma Nu's pride and joy ... star forward on student council basketball team ... Foresters' prexy.

CARMEN LEIGH: Red headed Chi O from B.A.C. ... "Sparky" to her friends ... coaches high school debaters ... Aggie varsity debater ... has uncontrollable love for bubble baths, people debaters, and novel beads ... Alpha Sigma Nu ... B.A.C. Club International Relations Club ... majored in commerce.

RAYMOND "BUTCH" KIMBALL: B.A.C. student body president Blue Key ... student council ... Alpha Sigma Nu ... Ag Econ club ... International Relations Club ... claims he likes Beeman's gum, dirty politics, attractive but intelligent women, banana splits and spring weather.

In Denver, Colorado, for a debate meet. Butch and Carmen at left, their partners and coach to right.

Left to right: Jack Caine, Carmen Leigh, Keith Sorenson, Eccles Caine.

Harold as student-body president, Utah State University.

Above: *Foresters'
Ball, 1941.
Harold and
Carmen, second
couple from left.*

Right: *Carmen's
graduation photo.*

CHAPTER 2

Real Life Begins

LOGAN, UTAH. JUNE 12, 1941,
ON STUDENT BODY STATIONERY

Dear Sparky,

I got your letter, and I followed your instructions. I put it in my trunk, and when I get to wherever I'm going, I'll read it.

I went to Salt Lake last Tuesday, and as far as they know, I will not be ordered to duty until I go to Philadelphia in September. However, in about two weeks I have to go to Denver to take my final physical. I am quite sure of passing it, and if I do, I'm all set for the big push. Boy, I'll surely be glad to know for sure. I received word yesterday that the Major General commandant had accepted my nomination as principal subject of course, if I pass the physical.

I wanted to thank you again for all the pleasant times we've had together during the past year. I really believe I gained more from that year than all the other four years of college put together. It was great. I wouldn't have missed it for a lot.

As soon as I am stationed, I'll write. The best of luck to you, Sparky, and I hope you like your new job. Sincerely, Harold

Dear Diary,

All I know about my new job is where my room will be

15

in the fancy new high school. I will be on the second floor, next to Horace Wilson, the new Industrial Arts teacher. He is a first-year teacher and a newlywed. I'm shocked to learn his salary will be larger than mine. The reason given is that he's married. I think the real reason is that he's a man.

School won't start for another three months, and I've already started my summer job as a waitress in the Zion Canyon Lodge. Part of the job is to join the other employees and welcome all incoming buses with traditional park songs. In the evenings, we entertain the "dudes" with a talent show, and when the buses depart we send them off with good-bye songs. The tour bus drivers are all young college men or just-out-of-college men who want to make the Forest Service their career. They look spiffy in the park uniform and have lots of time off between runs, as do the waitresses on split-shift—so, after work is FUN! Part of my job, for which I receive extra pay, is to help organize and M.C. the evening enter-tainment. Piece of cake for me. The base pay isn't much, but we get our board and room, and the tips in the lodge dining room are good. Most of all, it's a pleasant way to spend the summer.

Phillip Stuart, the night clerk on the desk, is giving me a big rush but, like college, I'm going to play the field. With all these cute bus drivers coming and going, who wants to be tied down to a guy who has to work nights?

I've no intention of getting serious with anyone. The only person I might be serious about isn't here, so that's it! I can't believe my poor timing—or is it bad luck? For the last two summers, when I didn't really know him, Harold was Range Examiner in Southern Utah and was based in Cedar City. Now I know him, but because of the darn war that's coming, he's decided to work in Pocatello this summer so he can spend some time with his parents. Between school and sum-mer jobs he's been home very little for the last five years. I can understand that, but if he were going to be in Cedar City, I'd have stayed there for sure. When I start teaching in Sep-tember, he'll be reporting to Marine Corps Basic School and I may never see him again. At least, for now, he calls occa-sionally.

The best job available in Pocatello for the summer is in the Alt Heidelberg Brewery. It's a one-man job and perfect for a young man who wants to be in top physical shape for entry into the Marine Corps.

The crew in front of the assembly line starts an hour before the other crews, because it takes an hour for the beer to get through the sterilizer. Harold's job is at the end of the assembly line. When the beer comes off the line, he puts an excise tax label on each case, loads twelve cases on a four-wheel handcart, pushes it into a self-service elevator to the second floor, down a long corridor, stacks the cases as high as he can reach, then runs the empty cart all the way back and catches up with the accumulation of cases coming off the conveyor belt.

It's like shoveling against the tide. It's impossible to take a break until the front crew takes theirs, halfway through the morning shift, again at noon, and then again halfway through the afternoon shift when the flow from the other end ceases. The crews are allowed fifteen-minute breaks morning and afternoon, and an hour break for lunch.

The recreation room is equipped with a stainless steel sink with two faucets, one dispensing cold water and the other cold draft beer. Harold had never had an alcoholic drink of any kind. For two days he tried without success to quench his thirst with water ... after five minutes back on the job, he would spit cotton. The third day he attacked the beer sink, laced it generously with salt, and found the answer to his survival on the job.

I like my classroom, and I'm glad it's a corner room on the top floor. You can see the red hills on one side and the college football field on the other.

While I was getting things set up for the opening day of school, the football coach called on me. He'd been having pre-season football practice, and he thought he should warn me that, according to the grapevine, practically the entire football squad was planning to register for my drama class.

"They're good kids," he assured me, "but they might be a handful. I'd advise you to be tough with them. From what I hear in the locker room, most of them think drama will be a snap class. Some of them think you're cute."

On the first day of school, I was pleased to see some attractive, obviously gregarious girls come into the room. Most looked eager and are the type you'd expect to see in a drama class. Then the boys started drifting in. They chose the chairs in the back of the room and looked a little ill at ease as they slouched, sitting more on their backbones than on what nature intended. Each seemed to be peering at me from under hooded eyes. No doubt this was the football team.

"Well, this is a surprise—a pleasant surprise. I see in front of me an abundant pool of leading men and ladies, character actors and actresses, and strong stage hands. We're going to learn to do everything required to put on a polished stage production. *Everyone* will participate. There will be no volunteers—there will be assignments. What you are asked to do, you'll do. If you are assigned to be the leading lady or leading man, you will do that. If you are assigned to do the stage makeup, you'll do that." The boys' eyes popped open in shock. "MAKEUP!"

"But first we'll learn good posture." The girls smiled and maintained their perfect stage presence. The boys reluctantly sat up straight.

"Now—we're going to have fun in this class. That is, those who can take it. Contrary to what you might have heard, this will not be an easy class. As you know, I haven't taken the class roll. Now that you have heard the ground rules, I'm going into my office for five minutes. Anyone who cares to do so may leave and change their registration. Those who stay will be more than welcome."

I departed for my office and listened intently, half expecting to hear the sounds of a mass exodus. When I returned, one boy had left. The only other change was that David Urie now sat at one of the front desks.

At the end of the day, I was exhausted. The first day on any new job is tough. I took off my shoes and leaned back in my swivel chair. Maybe I should wear sensible shoes, not high heels. Nawwwww.

My thoughts turned to Harold, who would be experiencing his first days in Marine Corps Basic School. Even though he was already a commissioned officer in the army, I'm sure indoctrination in the Marine Corps will be tough. I wonder how he's making out? He won't be the top man in the outfit as he was in college—he'll be just another greenhorn who will have to prove himself.

On September 2, 1941, his brief career in the brewery ended, Harold, in top physical condition, reported to Capt. Sam D. Puller at the Philadelphia Navy Yard. He placed the suitcase his sister gave him for graduation on the floor and walked briskly to the desk, bare-headed and dressed in a tweed suit, and snapped a crisp salute.

Captain Puller, tough and wiry with a medium build, leathery skin, and close-cropped head, looked up from his desk with the coldest blue eyes Harold had ever seen. His voice cut the air like a sharp knife, and he barked, "What school you from, lad?"

"I'm from Utah State ... sir."

"In the fust place, we don't salute in the Marine Corps *uncovered*. Now you get your ass outa here and report to the Sergeant Major down the hail."

Harold grabbed his new luggage on the run with such force that he found himself with the handle in his hand and the bag still sitting on the floor. He had no alternative but to go back and pick it up.

Captain Puller, he soon learned, was also his platoon drill instructor. Every time he walked the line, eyeing the new men with those ice blue eyes, his presence was so electric that Harold could feel the hair rising on the back of his neck.

"TORA, TORA, TORA!"

It is 7:53 A.M. Sunday, December 7, 1941, when Cmdr. Mitsuo Fuchida radios the code words "Tiger, Tiger, Tiger," notifying the Japanese navy that complete surprise has been achieved for Japan's attack on Pearl Harbor.

The clock shows 7:58 when Lt. Cmdr. Logan C. Ramsey races into the radio room at Ford Island, Hawaii, and orders the following message sent to U.S. forces:

"Air raid on Pearl Harbor, this is no drill!"

One hour and fifty minutes later, the United States Pacific Fleet and virtually every military installation on Oahu lies devastated from relentless torpedo strikes, divebombings, and strafing.

The toll: 2,403 Americans dead, another 1,178 wounded; 18 ships sunk or severely damaged; 188 warplanes destroyed, 159 damaged.

Nearly half of the dead, 1,177, died on the USS *Arizona* ... the highest loss of life on one ship in U.S. naval history.

The next day, President Franklin D. Roosevelt tells a stunned, shocked, but united America that December 7, 1941, "will live in infamy."

DECEMBER 7, 1941

Dear Diary,

I'm in shock! I've believed for the last two years that our country would be drawn into war. I never dreamed it would be like this ... a sneak attack, with no declaration of war. Our fleet is all but destroyed, and with an incredible loss of life. The news came over the radio while I was walking up the stairs to my room. I'm sitting on my bed, and all I can think of is my brothers, cousins, Harold, and all the other guys I know and don't know out there who'll be doing the fighting. My brother Ham is on an army transport on its way to the Phillipines. I wonder if they'll even get there?

For the last four years, lend-lease to Europe, the pros and cons of isolationism, and the feasibility of selling scrap metal to Japan have been topics of debate in our universities. I realize college students are seen by many as idealistic kids who think they know everything, but the consensus reached by them and their professors was that the U.S. could no longer depend on two oceans to shield the country from the dictators and imperial dynasties in our modern world. Isolationism is no longer possible and is downright dangerous! Not only does it breed a false feeling of security, but it affects our country's preparedness for war.

Anyone who has gone to the movies and seen the Movietone newsreels with that madman Hitler reviewing his goose stepping, swastika-bedecked troops, stretching as far as the eye can see in Germany, and the Fascist Mussolini doing the same in Italy, can't help but realize that they are a threat to the entire world. These two are allies, and other countries are joining them or being overrun and subjugated. We even hear rumors, unconfirmed, so far, that the Nazis are killing Jews and Gypsies in Poland. How can we say this is no concern of ours?

Emperor Hirohito in Japan rules by "divine right of birth." His subjects believe dying for the emperor is an honor and assures entry into heaven. Such fanaticism makes them a dangerous enemy, as we learned today. As many suspected, Japan is not to be trusted. The scrap metal and other materials sold to them came back to us today in the form of bullets.

Where have our leaders been? Obviously, with their heads in the sand, for surely they've had information the public hasn't. How could they not have been able to anticipate and prevent such an attack? It's the same old story, OLD MEN HESITATE AND YOUNG MEN DIE!

FEBRUARY 8, 1942,
WORT HOTEL, JACKSON, WYOMING

Hello Sparky,

I sincerely hope I have not been excommunicated as I so richly deserve. I kept your letter until I got to Philadelphia last September, and it was deeply appreciated. I also enjoyed your card and note very much at Christmas time. I am a lug, etc., for not answering sooner. I have been damned busy, but that is not sufficient excuse for my shortcomings. At any rate I hope you'll forgive me. Here goes.

Our school started in Philadelphia on September 15, and it ended on January 31. They gave us the most intensive course you could imagine, and I believe we are now well-qualified to lead our men in Uncle Sam's crack branch of the service. Yes, I'm really sold on the Marine Corps, now more than ever. It's really tops, and I'm proud to belong. Honestly received my greatest surprise of several years at our graduation when they read the names of the four high men in our class of 95, and I ranked third. Surely made the old blood proud!

During the time we were in school, we got relatively little leave, but, on the whole, I enjoyed the stay there very much. We had a great bunch of boys. My two friends and I spent our time seeing the latest shows and finding the best places to eat. Great sport! Would recommend highly *The Man Who Came to Dinner* and *Ball of Fire*. Both are plenty OK.

Dear Diary,

I couldn't believe what I was reading. The Utah Music Arts is presenting *The Man Who Came To Dinner* this season, and I'm playing the role of Lorraine Sheldon, the movie star.

What a coincidence. I love it. Boy, is this play going to cause a stir in Southern Utah.

We got down to New York for one weekend. Sparky, that's really a grand city. I saw everything from soup to nuts. Reminds me of San Francisco in atmosphere. Both have a lot of city in a small area.

We also got down into the southern states on maneuvers shortly after Christmas. Cold as hell, but we learned a lot and saw some new country. Managed to get home Christmas for four days. (Sure wish there were airlines flying into Cedar so I could whip down and see you—time is too short to drive.)

I figured then that it was probably our last leave for some time, but here I am again. I am now en route to duty in San Diego. Great, huh? Just the station I wanted. Of course, I don't know how long I'll be there, but at least I'm started in the right direction. My brother Jim is working there in a plane factory, so I hope we get a couple of months together. I know this is my last leave, so I'm making the most of it. Got into Pocatello Tuesday. Leave on the coming Friday. Got down to school for the Buzzer Ball Friday. My sister and I went dancing in Sun Valley on Labor Days and until Friday that was the only time I'd been dancing since you and I went to our Sigma Nu Spring Formal on May 10th. I damned near petrified. At any rate, I surely enjoyed the dance and my friends. We are now here in Jackson Hole on a two-day trip. Country's beautiful as ever.

Well, Sparky, if I haven't added insult to injury with this atrocious "penmanship" (the irony of that), I'd like very much to hear from you. How is teaching, our friends, and life in general? I'm sure it's treating you well—it always will I believe. My address, for the present, at least, is: Lt. H.L. Hiner, USMC Marine Corps Base, San Diego, California. Best of luck, Sparky, and my very best regards, Harold

Dear Diary,

It's great to hear from Harold. It doesn't surprise me he was third in his class ... cream always rises to the top. Wonder how his social life is? He doesn't say much about it, but then there's no reason why he should. With what he has facing him, I think he's entitled to fun wherever he can find it. He always tells me to have fun, but that's not easy now we're at war and all of the good men are places they would rather not be.

It's hard to believe I've been a schoolteacher for five months. I'm teaching history, literature, speech, and drama. I'm busy rehearsing for the high school play. My kids are great, and I think they're loving it. So much has happened, it seems I've been teaching forever.

I've never seen this country so united. Almost every man, woman, and child is behind the war effort. Most young men who were not already in some branch of the service are volunteering. Draft dodgers are considered cowards and shunned. Civilians, old and young, are doing whatever they can to help. The oceans, no longer a safety net, are now a battleground, and already enemy submarines have been spotted off the East and West coasts.

I enjoy teaching, and I think I'm a good teacher. I LOVE acting in the Music Arts plays and directing the high school play and coaching the debate team and don't even mind being in charge of all the assemblies. But I resent doing all this while teaching a full schedule of classes and being paid less than the men who teach classes from 9 to 4 and then go home. If I weren't living with my parents, I couldn't support myself.

My social life is mainly with the other teachers, who are older and married. I did meet a rather nice young guy by the name of Russell Price, whom I was dating. He represents some manufacturer of farm products and travels around the southern part of the state. I wonder why he isn't in the service but figure it's none of my business. It was over when, out of the blue, he told me he was buying an engagement ring at Bush Jewelers for me and hoped I'd accept it. I suspect he's trying to dodge the draft. I hardly know the guy.

Harold graduates from Marine Corps Basic School, Quantico, Virginia.

USS Boise officers, guests, and hosts of Variety Post American Legion of Philadelphia at the preview of The Navy Comes Through, *December 3, 1942. Harold first row, at left, probably telling a joke.*

High school teacher Carmen, with the school play cast and crew.

CHAPTER 3

Combat

FEBRUARY 23, 1942
LT. H. L. HINER, USMC
1ST GUARD CO. GUARD
BN. MARINE CORPS BASE
SAN DIEGO, CALIFORNIA

Dear Sparky,

Wouldn't that be great! I'd truly like nothing better than to be able to turn the old clock back and take you dancing again. However, since that's impossible, let's look ahead—let's do it sometime in the future instead. Down here, we are living from one day to the next. We have no idea how long we will be here; but if we are still here by the time school lets out—as we may easily be—I can think of nothing nicer than having you come through this neck of the woods. Let's hope.

It sounds to me as if you are having quite a busy and interesting time. I'm glad you concur in regard to *The Man Who Came to Dinner*. I enjoyed it tremendously. The dialogue is really clever. I would like very much to see your production. And, yes—I *can* imagine you in the role of a vamp. I'm not surprised to hear that you're tired of Cedar—it's a swell little city, and I enjoyed my two summers' work there, but your abilities overreach schoolteaching in Cedar.

Well, everything's OK on this end. I met my roommate in Ogden and we had a hilarious time from there out. He's a triple fraternity brother of mine from South Dakota and really a swell egg.

We stayed at the base in the transient officers quarters until last night. However, it was not required of us to live at the base and, inasmuch as we were drawing quarters allowance, four of us decided to take an apartment. Two I ran around with in Phila. and the other one is a swell southerner who also was in our class at Basic School. Boy, the apartment's really a dream. After you've been living in barracks as long as we have, you surely appreciate some place you can relax. One doesn't appreciate "home" until he no longer has one. I like the service very much, and my duty at the base is excellent. The base itself is absolutely beautiful. In peacetime, it must be heavenly. So long, Sparky. The best to you. Harold

MARCH 15, 1942,
SAN DIEGO, CALIFORNIA

Dear Sparky,

You lucky kid! So you got in on the Military Ball. I was hoping to, and I guess I would have made it if they hadn't shortened our course an additional two weeks. You're right when you say Pete is as crazy as ever—they ought to call him Looney instead of Tooney.

I don't doubt that your students are a cute bunch of little devils. Youth is ever subject to environment, don't you know? Furthermore, do you know that I'd like to enter the competition for that date at Provo? Think I'd stand a chance?

Speaking of duty, we Junior Officers in this battalion are getting a full ration of that these days. We are on two duty rosters and, consequently, stand eight days (and nights) duty out of every fifteen, which is plenty of duty. Take it from me! Oh well, it's all part of the game.

As concerns that little gal down here I'm supposed to beware of, I haven't run into her yet—damn it. This is really a serviceman's town. Actually, when you go to town, you see more uniforms—Marine, "a"rmy and "n"avy—than you do civvies, there is a dearth of women. Of course, there are plenty of a type, but we haven't been here long enough to meet the right kind of people. Consequently, I haven't had a date here yet. However, I haven't given up hope.

I find your news very interesting. "I don't know what to tell you." Marge and Abbott are in love, huh? Well, I guess most good men have a crazy streak in them somewhere. He must like the helpless type.

Where is Butcher Boy? I'm going to write him tonight at Kanosh. I've owed him a couple of letters for ages, so if that isn't the right place to write, will you please give me his address and give him my regards the next time you write him? What a lad! Surely hope he gets into the Navy Supply Corps. I'd hate to see all that brilliance wasted in the mud.

I can surely appreciate your dilemma. I'm glad to be started into what I believe now will be my life work. It's great to have that feeling of permanence and to know that you can direct all your energies to one end. I'm a firm believer in living in the present and in crossing bridges as I come to them. Have fun, best of luck. Harold

APRIL 8, 1942
MARINE CORPS BASE, SAN DIEGO, CALIF.

Hello Sparky,

Here goes! Thanks a million for your letter of the 28th. I surely enjoyed it. It's great to get that news from school. Glad to hear Kid Corey has hung his pin. Personally, it looks to me as if the Sigma Nu's are getting on the ball. I always did think the Chi O's were by far the best bet—or perhaps that was apparent.

I enjoyed seeing Crockett and Clinkinbeard again. They got in here a week ago yesterday, and I spent all day Thursday with them.

Got the best news I've heard for some time the other night when I ran into a Logan Army officer who told me it was quite certain that Elkins and Major Balch are now in Australia. Whoopee!!! I was afraid they were both in Bataan. Thank the

Lord they're not. May be seeing Elkins soon. Yes, Carmen, I've been detached from the base and am standing by for sea duty. I have received orders to my ship (incidentally a good new one) and am now waiting only for transportation to it. I'm all packed and ready to go on two hours' notice. I'll be at sea for the duration. Should be very interesting duty. It will be entirely different from anything I've ever done before, but it will be clean and exciting. I don't know just what my new mailing address will be as yet, so if you write before you hear from me, send it to 753 West Lewis, Pocatello, and my folks will forward it to me.

Well, Carmen, guess I'll be seeing action before long now.

Sort of glad. Know that I'll be aboard a crack unit and that we'll give a good account of ourselves. Take care of yourself. The very best for you. Be seeing you, Love, Harold

---

The USS *Boise*, only three years old and considered one of the fastest ships in her class, is equipped with new, top-secret radar. The radar can spot the enemy more than eight miles away and improves firing accuracy ten times. She has already been deployed with units of Task Force 5 to convey and protect important Allied shipping around the Phillipines and elsewhere in the Pacific. Though combat is heavy in the area, the *Boise* always seems to just barely miss the heavy action. To the crew's embarrassment, they have heard their ship referred to as the "Reluctant Dragon" by sailors from other ships.

Three of the *Boise* turrets have E's on their thick sides—navy recognition of a ship's excellence in gunnery. Every man aboard hopes to test the *Boise*'s gunnery skill in action before any of the other ships in her class. But here they are, steaming through the Golden Gate, heading for Mare Island, where the only action will be on the beach. According to the latest scuttlebutt, they are putting in here to pick up new personnel.

Ensigns Ted Balis and Brick Brafford, and Marine 2nd Lt. Harold Hiner became acquainted while waiting on the pier to report to the *Boise*. Aboard, they like what they see. A clean, well-squared-away ship, sharp-looking men, and a captain whose reputation is impeccable. "Iron Mike" Moran, a man well known for his ability to judge speed and distance . . . and for his iron-hand, velvet-glove policy of training his fighting men.

The men who rate liberty cards are already on deck in their best blues, ready to go over the side. Some of the marines in the *Boise*'s detachment are lined up there, too, their trouser creases razor-sharp.

Later, at one of the bars near the waterfront, a bunch of the *Boise* men, mostly marines, are whooping it up at one end of the bar lined solid with servicemen. At the other end is another group of sailors, who have been there for a long time, noisily stowing away beer.

One of the group, looking down the bar, raises his voice. "Well, look who's here. So, they're from the *Boise*—yeh, I know, the Hollywood sailors!" Others take it up, adding their own insulting comments.

Mike Moran's men calmly put down their glasses and form into a flying wedge of marines and sailors that snowplows into the bunch at the other end of the bar. It's a doozie of a brawl. As usual, the marines land promptly, and the *Boise* sailors are right with them. They land socko punches, right and left jabs, and haymakers coming all the way up from the bar rail. Blows are returned, but they are halfhearted, and the battle is soon over. The *Boise* men go back to finish their drinks, and that is the last time mention is made of Hollywood sailors in reference to the *Boise*. Their skipper, Iron Mike Moran—the fighting Irishman—would approve.

The following day, the USS *Boise* departs for Pearl Harbor and on July 27, 1942, sails unescorted for destination unknown. They are alone. Day after day they pass Pacific islands already in the hands of the Japanese. One of them is Midway, blackened by the terrible battle fought there not long before, a tiny sandspit no more than twenty feet above the level of the ocean. Early the next morning, the *Boise* is briefly escorted by two P.T. boats, then once again left all alone.

Marine 2nd Lt. Harold Hiner and several naval officers have duty on the bridge when the crew is called to General Quarters. This is the prearranged time for the captain to open and read the sealed orders.

The *Boise* is ordered to sail alone past Japanese-held Wake Island and continue toward Tokyo, attacking any enemy ships encountered. Its purpose is to divert attention and troops back to Japan and away from the Guadalcanal-Tulagi Island in preparation for the landing scheduled for August 7. If they come within 600 miles of Tokyo without encountering the enemy, they are to launch their two OS2U planes piloted by senior aviators Wallenberg and Boales. These planes are to proceed toward Japan, and if ships are spotted, radio the *Boise* to attack. If nothing is found, the planes are to continue to fly westward another fifty miles and attack any ships spotted by dropping the two 150-pound bombs each carries. Orders are to show no lights and to maintain radio silence.

When no enemy ships are seen, the planes take off on a cloudy afternoon. Two hours later, when they fail to return on time, the pilots break radio silence. They have lost each other in the soupy sky and are unable to locate the ship. Immediately, Radio Tokyo goes off the air, and the *Boise* knows they have been discovered.

The pilots contact the ship, asking for directions, and Moran orders them to return. The only means of navigation the pilots have is by dead reckoning, which is nothing more than a chart in their lap used to estimate wind and direction by the white caps in the ocean. When the planes fail to return, Moran radios them to drop their bombs so the ship can locate and retrieve them. There is no response.

Moran decides to make a last desperate attempt to bring them in. Whirling their two big searchlights around like drunken sailors on a 10,000-ton motorboat, the *Boise* goes to flank speed of thirty knots. The search continues for an hour and a half until it becomes obvious that the planes are unable to return and would by then be out of gas. Orders are given to cut and run.

Captain Moran knows his ship is being followed by a submarine that expects to be led to the rest of a task force. He knows they must lose the sub if they are to survive. Thanks to the darkness and the choppy water—and the wild maneuvers of Moran, who is reputed to be able to sail a ship as easily as ride a bicycle—they lose the submarine. However, they still have to sail back around the Japanese-held Wake Island and its land-based aircraft for another two days or longer. The lucky *Boise* sails at top speed and gets away.

When the men of the *Boise* get back to Pearl Harbor, they know they are a lucky ship, for without a doubt, this was a suicide mission.

With the Japanese controlling so many of the Pacific Islands, the success of the Guadalcanal operation had been deemed vital to the Allies.

The Doolittle Raid had already shaken the Japanese confidence. So, when a United States capitol ship of 1,100 men was discovered within 200 miles of Tokyo, they were convinced it would not be out there alone but would rendezvous with a major task force headed for their mainland. As a result, Japan withdrew all her carriers in order to protect Tokyo, and the landing of reinforcements on Guadalcanal by the Allies was accomplished.

Guadalcanal was a costly, brutal campaign, but would have been much worse, and perhaps unsuccessful, if air support had been used by the Japanese forces there.

When the *Boise* returns to Pearl Harbor, Lieutenant Hiner and Ensign Balis go on liberty together. Balis invites Hiner to accompany him to Naval Intelligence, where he hopes to call on Captain Momsen, the father of his Annapolis roommate. When they arrive, these still-wet-behind-the-ears shave-tails are surprised to be ushered into Momsen's office with all the respect and fanfare accorded visiting admirals.

Momsen greets them warmly and verifies that the *Boise* was followed for several days by a large submarine, which could have torpedoed them at any time. When the ship resorted to its crazy gyrations to find its aviators, the sub couldn't keep up. Luck rode with the *Boise* as it sailed back around Wake Island. Momsen admits there were tense days at Headquarters while monitoring the *Boise*'s progress.

As time goes by, the *Boise* becomes known as "the Black Phantom of Tokyo" and "the Ghost of the Pacific." Tokyo mistakenly reports the *Boise* sunk four times.

———— 🎺 ————

Dear Diary,

I haven't heard from Harold since his letter of April 8th.

The news from the Pacific is horrible. All we hear about are Japanese victories. The latest being "the First Battle of the Savo Sea," which was a bloody disaster for us. The U.S. fleet has still not recovered from the mortal blow struck at Pearl Harbor, and the country is frantically trying to catch up with the production of arms, ships, and all the accouterments of war. Our men are having to storm beaches without enough ammunition. Unconscionable!!

The only good news I've heard lately is that Butch was accepted in the Navy Supply Corps, a safe duty compared to most these days, though there's always the chance of a submarine attack. He called to tell me he has his commission. He has three days at home on his way to San Francisco to report for duty and wants me to come to Kanosh ... says he's been wanting to talk to me and wants me to meet his parents. It's only an hour's bus ride, and I'm looking forward to seeing him.

Gosh, he looks good. Same sweet, funny guy. His mother showed me to my room then his parents disappeared and left us alone. Butch filled me in on the news ... the only sad part is that Max Clinkinbeard has been reported killed in action. First time I've heard that about someone I know. It's awful!

"Sparky, I can't tell you how much I appreciate your coming. Time is short, but it didn't make sense to be this close and not see you." He gave me a bear hug and a rain of kisses, which surprised me, as our meetings of the last two years have been pretty casual.

We talked about the things we've done together. The travel with the debate squad, and how, when we were partners, we always knew the exact minute when we were winning. We'd catch each other's eye and send the signal. How we loved dancing together ... we thought we were the best jitterbug partners in the state of Utah, and the fun of campaigning and running for office ... and winning, of course. I realized he is the best friend I've had for the last five years, guy or girl.

"Sparky, I'm ready to take the next big step in my life. My

duty will allow me to be stateside frequently and I need to know how things are with us." This wasn't what I had expected, but I shouldn't have been surprised. I'd taken it for granted Butch would always be there ... as a friend, or more. Suddenly I realized there comes a time when you have to make a choice and, once it is made, the future is forever altered ... for better or worse. I wasn't prepared for this "moment of truth."

After hours of catching up, that moment could no longer be delayed. "Sparky, is it Hiner?"

"I don't know," is all I could say. He'd caught me off guard; I really didn't know. Two years ago it would have been different. Everything made sense then. Now nothing does.

I love Butch as I have since our first year in college, but I wonder, is there a difference between loving someone and "being in love"? I'm beginning to think there is.

Eventually we fell asleep on the couch, his arms around me, my head on his chest.

I cried on the way home ... I had lost something irreplaceable. We will always be friends, but it won't be the same once he has a wife, which I'm sure will be soon. Probably will be that cute little Kappa Delta, I think Adrus is her name. She's really nice ... I must be crazy!

On August 15, 1942, the *Boise* departs Pearl Harbor as escort commander of a convoy bound for Suva, Fiji Islands, the New Hebrides, and Vila, Efate. On September 6, she is ordered to proceed to Espiritu Santo for duty with Task Force 64. On September 18, she supports the landing of the U.S. Seventh Marines on Guadalcanal as reinforcements for the garrison already there. The *Boise* returns to Espiritu Santo on the 21st.

Task Force 64 puts to sea once again on October 6, 1942, on a raiding mission off Guadalcanal. Its purpose is to break up the "Tokyo Express," which is, almost nightly, delivering reinforcements and supplies to the Japanese at Cape Esperance. From early reconnaissance reports on October 11, it is evident that enemy targets will be in the area that night. The *Boise*, a light cruiser, is the last ship in a column of three other cruisers, the *San Francisco*, the *Helena*, and the *Salt Lake City*, and five destroyers.

The task group's course is set for a point just off Cape Esperance, on the northern tip of Guadalcanal. It is a moonless night, which gives the Japanese a perfect opportunity to sneak in their ships and troop reinforcements. The same black cloak covers the movements of the *Boise*'s task group and, as the men topside stand at their battle stations, they can barely make out the silhouettes of the other ships around them. There is no sound in all the darkness except for the hiss and wash of the water split by the *Boise*'s prow, and the hum of her powerful machinery far below.

In a lofty perch abaft (behind) the bridge, Sam Forter, a young lieutenant only two years out of Annapolis, presides over the forward director of the main battery. The turret officers are alert, waiting to hear the command "Commence firing." The men stationed at the five-inch guns on the open deck are in the same expectant mood.

Over the headset phones, a soft chant is heard:

"Pass the word from gun to gun; this won't be a dummy run." The second loaders and ammunition-passers nervously shift their weight from one foot to the other as they talk in low tones. "Boy, this looks like our chance to get in some licks; come on, Yamamoto, bring on those ships."

Twenty minutes before midnight, Lieutenant Forter is still staring into the darkness when he sees a distant group of objects barely visible on the *Boise*'s starboard bow.

"On the target!" Sam speaks on his headset phone.

"How many ships?" Iron Mike's question is relayed through the gunnery officer.

"Seems to be five, sir." (There are six.)

"Pick out the biggest and commence firing!"

Lieutenant Hiner, commander of turret three, observes an instant tautening of nerve and muscle as Mike Moran's order is relayed to the pointers and trainers seated beside their guns. He is confident his marines are ready and will perform exactly as they should. Sure enough, the turrets shake as fifteen guns fire in a single tremendous blast, lunging backward in swift recoil before sliding forward again. Breeches fly open, the next shells are out of the hoist and rammed home with perfect timing, and again the turrets shake; this is the rhythm of fire for which these men have trained every day for so long.

Boise's first target is set afire and after several more hits from the *Boise*'s guns is seen to sink in four minutes. *Boise* then trains her guns on another enemy destroyer and sinks her within two minutes. Sixty seconds later, *Boise* engages a two-stack Japanese cruiser and sets it afire. Contact lasts for four minutes, during which time *Boise* sustains a hit by one eight-inch and several five-inch shells. The captain's cabin is demolished and set afire. Then *Boise*'s target explodes and disappears. Fires are observed on an enemy destroyer. *Boise* fires on it for two minutes until she sinks. *Boise* then attacks another Japanese ship on her starboard beam. Meanwhile, a Japanese heavy cruiser returns the *Boise*'s fire until it is blown up with an assist from the *Salt Lake City*.

Boise turrets one, two, and three are hit and set afire with heavy casualties. Lieutenant Hiner's crew continue firing even after the magazine is hit. By sheer force of will and bodily strength, they fire their guns in spite of slow recoils, until put out of action by a hit on the face plate and the flooding of their handling room. Lieutenant Hiner, with utter disregard for his own safety, orders his men out and stays behind to perform valuable service, relaying orders from the damaged turret to Damage Control Central.

When an enemy eight-inch shell rips into the *Boise*'s hull nine feet below the water line, her magazine explodes, killing three officers and 104 men (and along with other parts of the ship, wiping out Hiner's and Balis's stateroom). Her sister ships give her up for lost as flames engulf the entire ship.

The *Boise* withdraws from the column. Captain Moran and the crew swing into action—they flood the exploded magazine, put out the fires, plug the shell holes with bedding, and two hours later come steaming through the night at twenty knots to take their place in the task force.

Not a man in turret two is alive; some survivors in turret one get out with the help of Lieutenant Hiner and his marines. When turrets one and two are thought to be cleared of gas, Marine Lieutenant Hiner, described in the press as "a poker-straight blond boy from Pocatello, Idaho," and gunner Duncan lead the way into each in turn. A ghastly sight faces them, but they grit their teeth and remove the dead from the turrets.

Too badly damaged for further action, the *Boise* starts for the states. Still in enemy waters, they have to traverse "Torpedo Junction," where Japanese subs patrol. When the *Boise* finally reaches a friendly port, a destroyer pulls alongside, and while both ships keep under way, a bag of mail is passed over to the cruiser. Letters from home! Some pretty old, but all a joy to be read and re-read.

On the way home, the dead that can be reached are buried. As each name is called, the exec responds, "Absent." Four pallbearers then lift up one of the canvas bags and place it on a flag-draped platform at the ship's rail. The bag, weighted with a six-inch shell, is consigned to the sea.

"November 19, 1942, the 11,000-ton battle-scarred *Boise* docks at the Philadelphia Navy Yard, a year and a day since it departed for the Philippines. Patches cover a gaping hole in her hull, her tall mast is scorched by fire, blisters of paint bulge from her superstructure. Hundreds of shell fragments have scarred and pocked her, but she sails proud and unfaltering through the early morning haze. Riverboats toot their greeting, sailors swarm over the decks of adjoining ships to wave and shout at her, thousands of workmen set up a cheer as she moves slowly into her berth. As the first mooring line touches the pier, a navy band blares 'Hold that Tiger.' The Reluctant Dragon is no more." (In Morris's *Pick Out the Biggest*.)

OCTOBER 30, 1942
734 WEST LEWIS, POCATELLO, IDAHO

Dear Carmen,

I was happy to find a letter from you when I returned home today from a trip with Mr. Hiner. Yes, Harold spoke of you often a year ago last summer when he was home.

Somehow it seems to bring him a little nearer tonight to hear from one of his friends I know he likes so much. James once told me of the girlfriends Harold had. He liked you the best, and James is quite critical. One of your letters came here, and I was happy to forward it.

The last time we heard from him was September 27th. It had been written September 4th. Said he was well and fine and had never been sea sick. He also said the only letters he had received were two from Mr. Hiner. We keep on writing and hoping he will get them sometime. So hope you will write him again— some of them may get through.

He never tells where he is, only at sea thousands of miles first one way then another. Last time he wrote he said he had only been ashore one afternoon since he left San Francisco. The address you have is correct: 2nd Lt. H. L. Hiner, USMC, U.S.S. Boise, c/o Fleet Post Office, San Francisco, Calif.

Love, Irene Hiner

Dear Diary,

The night of November 19, 1942, I was at the high school helping the other teachers handle the sugar rationing for the town. Halfway through the evening I saw my father walk in the door, still in his dirty work clothes, obviously just home from riding the range. He looked tired, as well he might, for he was having to handle all the ranch work with both Dick and Ham overseas. I looked at his face and knew something unusual had brought him here ... I feared we'd had bad news about one of my brothers.

He walked over to my table and his tired, worn face lit up in a smile when our eyes met. "Carmen, Harold Hiner's ship, the *Boise*, just limped into the Philadelphia Navy Yard all shot up. It came over the radio. They said twelve men had been awarded the Navy Cross for outstanding bravery under fire. Harold was one of them and the medal was not awarded posthumously, so he must be all right."

All that evening and the next morning, the radio and press reported the news of the *Boise*. They were called the "One Ship Fleet," as they had been primarily responsible for sinking six

Japanese ships in twenty-seven minutes. The next day, I received two telegrams:

HAROLD WIRED TONIGHT FROM PHILADELPHIA NAVY YARD THAT HE IS SAFE AND SOUND. HE IS TO PHONE US ON THE 25TH. LOVE, MR. AND MRS. LYLE HINER

HELLO SPARKY. HAVE BEEN RECEIVING ALL YOUR LETTERS SINCE WE ARRIVED. APPRECIATE THEM SO VERY MUCH. GOT YOUR LATEST TODAY. WILL ANSWER IMMEDIATELY. STAND BY. HAROLD. PHILADEL-PHIA, PA.

Ensign Raymond "Butch" Kimball

Top: *The crew and recipients of the Navy Cross.*

Center: *Harold receiving the Navy Cross.*

Bottom: *Harold (left) and crew on the* Boise *after the Savo Sea battle.*

Idahoans Will Patch Her Up With Bonds

MARINE CAPT. John W. Graves of Los Angeles puts his fist in one of the holes torn in the U.S.S. Boise by Japanese shell fragments as Marine Lt. Harold Hiner of Pocatello looks on. Hiner was decorated for heroism in the Southwest Pacific. Meanwhile, Lions clubs of Idaho are sponsoring statewide war bond drive for funds to aid in the repair of the heroic ship. A Lions club bond program will be presented at noon today at City Hall corner.

Newspaper clipping of Harold on the Boise.

Earns Plaudits

Lieutenant Harold L. Hiner . . .
Received congratulations from
Idaho governor on hero award.

Clark's Letter Lauds Idaho Hero on Boise

Parents of Marine Told of Son's Recent Promotion

Tribune Intermountain Wire

POCATELLO, Idaho— A letter from Governor Clark was received Saturday by Mr. and Mrs. Lyle Hiner of this city, expressing Idaho's "pride" in their son, Lieutenant Harold L. Hiner of the marines, decorated for bravery while serving aboard the "one-ship fleet" cruiser Boise.

At the same time they received a brief wire from their son, dated Philadelphia, which said simply:

"Arrived Philadelphia safe and sound. Telephone Wednesday night."

The telegram was signed: "First Lieutenant."

Father Proud

"I guess he got a promotion." Mr. Hiner said with more than a trace of pride. "He has been just a second lieutenant."

First Lieutenant Hiner, U S M C, was aboard the famed, tough bruiser when she wallowed into a fleet" of six Japanese warships, and, outnumbered and outgunned, was instrumental in sinking the half dozen Jap vessels.

Governor Clark's note said:

"I have just read of the decoration your son received in the line of duty and know how proud you are.

"As chief executive of the state of Idaho I wish to express to you the pride the state has in this news." Signed, Governor Chase A. Clark.

U S A C Graduate

The 24-year-old marine corps hero graduated from Utah State Agricultural college in June 1941.

He was one of 40 men selected in the nation to exchange reserve commissions for an active commission in the marine corps, joining that organization in September, 1941.

He also saw action in the Solomons, he has advised his parents.

Lieutenant Hiner was graduated from Utah State Agricultural college in 1941, where he was student body president and one of the most active men on the campus.

After graduating in 1936 from East High school in Salt Lake City, where he was active in football, orchestra, rifle team and R O T C, he entered U S A C in 1937, majoring in range management.

He served as president of the U S A C student body and of the Utah Foresters' club and was captain of the college rifle team in 1940-41. He won the highest R O T C award offered at the college in 1939-40 and was named regimental adjutant. He won the coveted college citizenship award in 1940-41. He was awarded a permanent commission in the U. S. marine corps upon graduation.

Prominent in scholarship, Lieutenant Hiner was a Phi Kappa Phi, natonal sholastic honorary fraternity; Blue Key, service honorary; Alpha Zeta, agricultural honorary, and Xi Sigma Pi, forestry honorary.

Newspaper clipping of Harold on the Boise.

Above: *Official USN Photo. USS Boise. Philadelphia Navy Yard, November 1942. Damage under Navigation Bridge. (Sailor Unknown)* —Courtesy U.S. Navy

Below: *Official USN Photo. USS Boise. Guadalcanal (Cape Esperance), October 1942. Temporary patch to hull, starboard side.* —Courtesy U.S. Navy

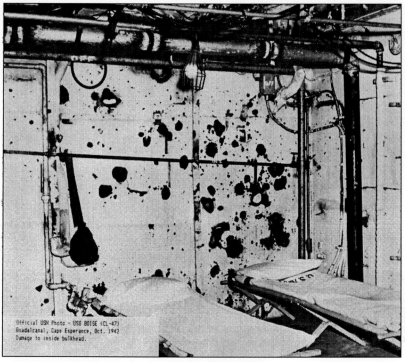

Official USN Photo - USS BOISE (CL-47)
Guadalcanal, Cape Esperance, Oct. 1942
Damage to inside bulkhead.

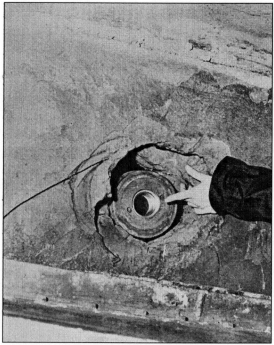

Above: *Official USN photo. USS Boise, Guadalcanal, Cape Esperance, October 1942. Damage to inside bulkhead.*

—Courtesy U.S. Navy

Left: *Official USN photo. Unexploded eight-inch Japanese shell in Turret #1 on USS Boise. Picture taken in Philadelphia Navy Yard, November 1942.*

—Courtesy U.S. Navy

CHAPTER 4

ℛeunion

1 DECEMBER, 1942
USS BOISE   CENSORED MAIL

Dear Carmen,

Hold your hat, gal, 'cause here goes! I'll see if I can catch up. To begin with, I received only one of your letters while we were down there, dated July 18. That arrived after the battle, and I knew we were coming back and that you'd receive my letter more quickly mailed from here. This is it. Then since our arrival, I have been receiving your delightful letters thick and fast. Apparently, as soon as they found we were returning, they started gathering our mail at Pearl Harbor to send to us, and I believe we have most of our back mail by now.

Sparky, with your usual wisdom, intuition I suppose you'd call it, you hit upon exactly the thing the boys in the service like most—news from home. Honestly, down there it is mail call, not pay call, that is the most eagerly awaited. Unlike the army and a certain class of ships, we keep moving so fast our mail just doesn't *catch up* with us. Occasionally, we *catch up* with some, and it's a day of rejoicing, indeed. So please keep writing.

So far it's a poor exchange for you, though, because I always found my own letters terribly dull before this strict censorship. Now, they are positively "godawful." However, with the male's normal selfishness, I shall continue to return my poor letters for your interesting ones for as long as you care to write.

47

It's really too bad, though, for we see so much—so many new and different places—and do so many exciting things that I believe even I could write an interesting letter, were it not for the strict rules of naval censorship.

Thanks for all the news of our friends. Please send me Butch's address when you write next. It's possible we might make arrangements to get together. Also please send Elkins' and I'll be sure to look him up when we get back to Pearl Harbor.

Hey, Sparky, what's the dope on your writing? For whom are you writing, and are you using your own name? Sounds great—tell me about it.

The *Iron County Record*, Cedar City's weekly paper, was looking for human-interest stories about the war. My mother, Beth, wrote a column about the local boys. I wrote a "then and now" piece about my last year in college and what was happening to the girls and guys now that the country is at war. After the local paper printed it, I was asked by the *Salt Lake Tribune* to participate with several others who are writing a joint column, featuring young people from Utah. It is primarily a "where are they now and what are they doing gossip column."

I call my segment "Under the Eaves" because so much of it originated from my days in the Chi O house.

Also, what's the latest development in the Wave situation? Are you going to be released from your contract or are you going to finish this school year? Yes, I've heard of the Waves, and they appear to be doing a fine job. Hope you get in soon, if that is what you want.

Well, guess I'd better knock off for now. Surely was glad to hear from you and my parents that you'd been corresponding. You're right—they are really swell. I believe I'm going to get 20 days' leave around the first of the year. More on that soon.

Write soon and I'll answer immediately. Until then, so long, Harold

---

DECEMBER 22, 1942
PHILADELPHIA NAVY YARD
CENSORED MAIL

Hello Sparky,

Received your last letter, and was it a honey. What would you give to go back to school with the old gang, in the same atmosphere, for a glorious Logan spring quarter? Priceless, and how!!

Say, Carmen, guess what: Near the end of last week, while I had the duty, someone called twice for me. When I got off, I hit for a phone, and it was none other than Handsome Harold Steed. We got together that evening for a "gab-fest" that would have rivaled yours and Alice's. I had more dope than he did—thanks to you. We had a wonderful time going to school all over again.

Yes, Carmen, I am getting leave starting on the 28th. Shall reach Pocatello on the 31st and will not have to start back until January 15th. Isn't that great? I would surely like to see you, too, but fear I cannot get down to Cedar City. I hope to run down to school sometime during my visit. I'll keep you posted. We'll work something out.

The writing sounds interesting. I shall keep an eye out for it—and "find out a lot of things I didn't know then."

Well, Sparky, it's nearly 2:00 A.M., so guess I'll hit my sack, as the Navy would say. I personally think that's a helluva vulgar way to refer to so luscious an item as a BED, but the Navy's too big for me to buck, so guess I'll simply turn in.

Goodnight, Carmen. A very Merry Christmas to you, and a new year filled with happiness. Harold

P.S. I saw "Carmen" presented here last week. It was lovely!

P.S. 2 I'll keep you posted as to how my leave works out.

JANUARY 3, 1943
JACKSON HOLE, WYOMING

Dear Carmen,

Hello, and thanks a million for that terrific special delivery letter. It arrived "home" one hour after I did. It was really sweet of you, and your timing was super.

Gad, it's great to be home! We made New Year's Day serve as Christmas for us. Then, yesterday morning, we packed our gear into the car and took off for Jackson Hole, Wyo. Here we are. Have you ever been up here, Sparky? I guess it's about my favorite country. There's about eight inches of snow on the level, and it's a winter wonderland for sure. (Just in case you've never seen this country, I'm sending you a postcard from here, too.) At any rate, Father and I took a long trek on our snow-shoes today and got some beautiful color movies. We'll do like-wise again tomorrow, and return to Pocatello the following day. This is really a soft life. I've missed the mountains more than anything at sea, for I really love them. However, I really like the sea, too. Quite a problem!

I expect to be down at school next Friday and to go on down to S.L. on Saturday. It'd be great if you failed to come this weekend as you'd planned and came next weekend instead. You see, you're not the only "wishful thinker."

Thanks for the news you sent. So, more of our friends are hitched? More power to them! Had a letter and picture from Corey and Betty. Cute kids, and are they happy! My sister and her husband are wonderfully happy, too. This marriage must be great stuff.

I'll keep my eyes open for "Under the Eaves." Catchy title! Besides, I'll always have a soft spot in my heart for the Chi O house and its occupants.

As concerns the Waves, I think they're a good outfit and are doing a good job, but for God's sake, steer clear of the Wac! They impress me as being mostly—a bunch of misguided old hens playing soldier. However, perhaps I'm wrong. At any rate, if you go into the Waves, I'll know they're O.K.

Well, guess I'd better "train in and secure" as the Navy says. I still hope, by some fluke we can work something out, so I can see you before I leave. Goodnight, Sparky. Harold

JAN. 6, 1943 (POSTCARD)
ROCK SPRINGS, WYOMING

Dear Sparky,
    Went snowshoeing all over this country shown here today. Really beautiful and as quiet in the timber as a cathedral. Harold

Why do I seem to be in the wrong place at the wrong time? When Harold worked in Cedar, we didn't know each other. Now I'm working here and we're in a war, no planes fly in or out. With gas rationed, you can't drive any distance, even if you have all the time in the world. Bus travel is a pain, but it's better than walking.

We talked on the phone, and I changed plans so we'll be in Salt Lake the same weekend. A substitute teacher will fill in, allowing me to stay over two days and investigate officer's training in the Waves. Thank goodness I have reservations at the Hotel Utah, where the navy is interviewing.

Harold wants me to meet Lyle and Irene. It's about time! I've been corresponding with them for at least a year. We'll have dinner in the Empire Room at the hotel. I'm sooooo excited!

The bus ride to Salt Lake seemed to take forever. I worried all the way, wondering if Harold would be disappointed. In the last year and a half he's had liberty in New York, Philadelphia, San Francisco, and San Diego, where I'm sure he dated. That's pretty tough competition for a country girl.

I arrived in Salt Lake early on purpose, so I could shop at "Makoffs" for a new dress. I found one I *really* like ... black with a lace insert at the neckline and a straight, short skirt. It does something for my minor assets—in an understated way of course, as do the gorgeous spike-heeled shoes I bought. Hope I look snazzy!

—————

Saturday Jan. 9, 1943 ... about 4:00 P.M. I can't sit still. Every
sound from the corridor outside my door makes my heart
pound like a hammer. Then if there is no knock on *my* door, I
feel let down. Finally, a knock on my door; the instant I saw his
face, I knew I needn't have worried ... he hasn't changed. He's
the same handsome, self-confident, nice, exciting guy. When he
put his arms around me, the worries, frustrations, and anxieties
of the last year and a half seemed trivial.

I've tried to think of him as just a good friend, which he
is ... just like Butch. I've been afraid to allow him to mean too
much to me ... now I'm afraid it's too late—he already does.
Boy, am I a fraidy-cat.

Dinner was elegant; Lyle and Irene are really nice. As soon
as dinner was over, they diplomatically suggested we take their
car and have fun. We took off for the Coconut Grove, where we
knew there would be dancing on Saturday night. Harold had
hoped we could "whip down to the Top of the Mark" in San
Francisco—his favorite spot. Not possible this time.

Hooray for dancing! Even in a huge ballroom filled with
strangers, we feel we're alone. The smooth, romantic music—
"Does Your Heart Beat for Me?" and "Lonesome" followed by
the other tunes we love—lured us so close to each other, the reality of war and separation faded in importance. These are moments in time that are worth living—that is enough for now.

We danced until midnight, loving the closeness ... appreci-
ating the privacy of the dimmed lights, not minding the shad-
owy figures—mostly servicemen and their girls—who, like us,
are lost in each other.

He apologized for the poor fit of his uniform, explaining
that his complete wardrobe of uniforms, including the classy
boat cape and dress sword, were destroyed by a direct hit on his
stateroom. He's still making payments to Horseman's Uniforms
for them and wearing a borrowed one until the new ones are
delivered. I think he looks WONDERFUL ... He says I'm
BEAUTIFUL!

—————

Early morning Sunday the 10th. After breakfast, we walked to the Temple grounds and listened to the Mormon Tabernacle Choir. Back to the hotel, where we can be alone, we tried to make the most of this time together. I'm disappointed to hear him say he doesn't believe the war will be over very soon. We talk about our friends who are married or planning to be. They appear to be happy, in spite of separations—some are even starting families.

I know how he feels about wartime marriage, and for good reasons. One of his duties aboard ship is to censor mail—he sees firsthand men torn apart when they receive a "Dear John" letter from a wife or girlfriend. I see young girls, married, left alone, usually pregnant, and then, worst of all, widowed. It is a tough choice to make. Nothing is as it should be, or as we thought it would be after college.

By noon it's time for him to leave. He took my hand in both of his. He has strong hands—often doesn't know his own strength. They are gentle as they close over mine. "Sparky, there's a difference in my situation and some of our friends. They are not regular army, navy, or marines. They are men who have volunteered or been drafted. The rules which apply to them are different for me. I'm a regular. When this is over, they will be sent home. Career officers will be retained as long as there's a job to be done. Some of them, like Butch, are in a position to be stateside frequently, and are not generally in combat as am I. It makes a difference in the choices they have." I wonder—does he know about my recent visit with Butch?

Why, of all the guys I know or meet, is this the one I can't seem to forget ... I must be crazy! Maybe it's because I trust him ... and perhaps something inside tells me this is the best man I'll ever know.

Everyone else I know is in a hurry. Most of the guys have the same line ... "I'm going overseas—I may never come back—live while you can." In other words—let's hop into bed. Even some of the girls are acting crazy. Some try to marry a guy going overseas so they will get an allotment: then they date because they're "soooo lonesome." It's a crazy time! When he kissed me good-bye, I wondered if I would ever see him again.

CENSORED MAIL

Dear Sparky,

Guess I'll have to print this—after a fashion—for the train is rocking too violently to write. I suppose by now I'm in discard anyway for failing to write Monday as I told you I would. Honestly, I'm sorry, but I have been quite busy getting ready for this return trip. Gad, but it's rough, Carmen! It's practically an insult to send you this scratching so if you tire of reading it, just chunk it into the circular file, and I'll have another one on the way before long.

Well, Carmen, you already know it, but I wanted to tell you anyway what a great time I had with you the other night. Just like old times! Incidentally, how do you like Coconut Grove? Personally, I think it's a swell place with the right girl. It's only too bad we couldn't whip down to the "Top of the Mark" Sunday night as we had planned. I'm convinced "War is hell!" At any rate, we did have fun, didn't we? In fact, Carmen, with you, I've never had other than a tip-top time. I've really got some nice memories of our dates stowed away.

Lord, Sparky, this scribbling is so terrible I'm going to quit. Please (note—we just stopped for a moment) give my regards to your folks. Here's hoping we get together again pretty soon. Have a good time. Write often, and I'll reciprocate. If you do go into the Waves, I hope with all my heart you are stationed where I may see you occasionally—or more often.

Good luck. Write, Harold

I'm taking this to Philly, as all our mail must be censored.

JANUARY 20, 1943
CENSORED MAIL

Dear Sparky,

It's after midnight, so just a short note to explain the other one. Came whipping out here yesterday morning and dropped my gear (including letter) off here at the barracks en route to the ship to report in. Got aboard and found I had the duty and couldn't get off, of course, until this afternoon. Consequently, this already late letter is later. The only reason I'm sending the sloppy thing at all is to show you I'm not quite so slow as it looks.

Again, Carmen, thanks so much for helping to make my leave so enjoyable. It really seemed like old times—or better— and they were swell.

Have only one little item of news tonight, but one which made me very happy. The present commanding officer of the marine detachment has been ordered elsewhere, so from now on, I'm the commanding officer of the detachment. My Junior officer (a 2nd Lt.) has already reported aboard and we're getting squared away. More later. Good night for now, Sparky. I'll write again in a few days. Harold

FEBRUARY 4TH, 1943
CENSORED MAIL

Dear Carmen,

I'm off—in answer to two delightful letters. Honestly, Sparky, I find your letters utterly charming. Would that I were so eloquent!

How long do you have before your play is to be presented? A week? I surely wish I could be there, for I've a good idea who'll steal the show. From what you tell me of your part, you must fill it to perfection. In fact, you must have relatively "little acting" to do to play it admirably. Yes, I would like the book when you're finished with it.

The Utah Music Arts is presenting the Broadway play *My Dear Children,* based on the life of John Barrymore. I'm playing the role of Cordelia, Barrymore's favorite daughter. We were in rehearsal for it prior to my trip to Salt Lake, and Harold was intrigued with the story.

No, Carmen, I have not read the *Conrad Argosy* and, yes, we do have room for such things aboard. We officers have staterooms with plenty of room for storage of personal gear. I must pick up some sort of a library before we shove off. Your OK is tops with me, and if you say the word, that's number one on my list. At long last I got to see *Random Harvest*. If you haven't it should be placed at the top of your "must" list.

As concerns the Waves, Carmen, I hardly know what to tell you. I can understand your parents' stand, of course. Nevertheless, the Waves seem to me to be much preferred to teaching—particularly since you are over-worked and underpaid. My main advice to you would be to worry less about it. In your last letter, you really sounded low. Don't forget there are thousands of people everywhere forced by the war to mark time. So go ahead and mark time until something you want opens up and then take it in a flash. Perhaps the Waves aren't the answer, but someplace there's a big job for a girl with your talents.

You mentioned you might be coming to N.Y. to see Carmen Croft in the spring. When might that be? It is practically spring here now. As you know, I can't guarantee anything, but I would surely like to be here for such a visit, and I will promise to stay here long enough to receive your valentine.

Well, Sparky, guess I'd better knock off and hit my sack as it is nearly 2:30. Good night, and don't worry too much. As ever, Harold

I passed the test and met the requirements for officer's training in the Waves. My parents are upset and my brothers horrified I would even consider it. I feel guilty for upsetting them when they are already under the stress of combat.

I'm going to think about it for a while, but I won't sign my teaching contract for next year until I look into other possibilities. Principal Wright says he will keep my contract open for as long as he possibly can, in case I change my mind. That's nice of him, but I don't think I will. I feel a need to get out of Cedar. I've been here all my life ... except for two years of college. I need a change and some challenge in my life.

Carmen when she met Harold in Salt Lake City
after the Savo Sea battle, January 1943.

Harold in full dress uniform.

Cast of the Music Arts play My Dear Children, *based on the life of John Barrymore. February 1943.*

CHAPTER V

Decisions, Decisions

Dear Diary,

I have a lot of catching up to do from being in Salt Lake. I talked to Harold on the phone before the *Boise* sailed, but so far no mail. I wonder where he's headed ... maybe it's just as well I don't know. The Music Arts' play is over; now I have to get rolling on the high school play and make a decision about the Waves, or what to do with my immediate future.

At least I have the play chosen and I'm excited about it. Grant Redford, who directs the college and community plays, has contacts I don't, and he helped me find a play worth the time and effort. In the midst of a world war, I can't see doing some dumb little-girl-meets-boy piece of fluff.

I've chosen *Letters to Lucerne*, now playing on Broadway. It depicts the dilemma of girls from the countries in Europe, brought together at a girls' school in neutral Switzerland. There, young people confront the realities of war and see the enemy in the faces of their lovers and friends. I'm at school by 9:00 A.M. and generally not home until 11:00 P.M.

More excitement, especially for the young girls, the college is now a pre-flight training school for air force cadets. It's the biggest news in town these days. I got my first look at them the day after I got back from Salt Lake.

The cadets take their meals at the Escalante Hotel, where they are housed. That means they are marching down the street as I walk along the sidewalk at noon and after school. They march in cadence and chant air force lingo or songs. The third day after my return, as they came alongside me, the drill instructor bellowed, *"EYES RIGHT."* The cadets chanted: "CHECK OUT THE LEGS. *EYES RIGHT* ... HOW 'BOUT A DATE? HUP ... TWO ... THREE ... FOUR." Each day since then, the chant has been a little bolder, and sometimes it's a mildly suggestive song. Invariably, some of my students are in the area and I can hear them snicker. I can't resist a peek, but I've never looked full at them. After all, teachers have to keep their dignity.

I have lunch at home or at the Candy Kitchen, where I used to work in the summers. Dorothy Harter owns the business with her brother, and we're friends. If she has more customers than she can manage, I help out. Two weeks after the cadets came to town, I decided to visit Dorothy after school, and when I got there, the place was so busy I grabbed an apron and took over the soda fountain. When I finished tying on the apron, I looked up and met the clear, blue eyes of a blonde, very good-looking cadet. "What may I do for you?" I stammered.

"Well, I'll have one of whatever you think is the best thing you make here."

"In my opinion that would be a root beer float. We make all our own ice cream ... it's the best." I could feel his eyes on me as I made the concoction, making sure to put an extra scoop of delicious chocolate ice cream in the root beer.

"Ummm, this *is* good, but don't you think I should be *richly* rewarded for all the undercover work I've done to track you down and find out where you live and where you go when we pass you by? A date would be a fitting reward."

"Well, I usually don't date someone I don't know or to whom I haven't been introduced."

He stood up—I could see he is tall enough—and extended his hand over the counter. "Allow me to introduce myself. I'm Art Culver, from Arcadia, California, and I've been checked out and my past thoroughly investigated by the Army Air Force. My motives are honorable." He held his hand in place until I offered mine.

"I'm—"

"I know, you're Carmen Leigh." He pronounced my last name, Lee. "I saw you in the play. Incidentally, I think you're wasting your talent in Cedar City. You were great! How about that date?"

I explained I was presently in rehearsal for the high school play, which takes most of my evenings. The next night he showed up at the school auditorium and waited for me to finish, then walked me home. He's nice, and I enjoy being with someone my own age. He does this almost every night, so when our car is available, I drive to the evening rehearsal and, if I finish early enough, we take in a movie.

Art, being a city boy, is enamored with our small town and thinks ranching is glamorous. He asked if I thought my dad would bring a couple of horses in from the ranch and let us take a horseback ride together. I put him off saying I was too busy rehearsing the play. The truth is, I'm a poor excuse for a rancher's daughter. I'm uncomfortable on a horse and avoid one whenever possible. Dad says you must let the horse know who's in charge ... in my case, it's the horse. I'm hoping Art will forget about it. I'm assuming he's an experienced equestrian, but I'm not, and I don't want to admit it.

FEBRUARY 18, 1943. CENSORED

Dear Carmen

At long last, here is an answer to your wonderful letter. Please forgive me—this time it could not be helped, for I've really been swamped as I shall explain later.

First, how did the play go? Superbly, I'm sure. Only wish I could have seen it. Tell me all about it the next time you write. Did you still persist in thinking of doing horrible things to your hero as he made love to you?

By now, I presume, you're well into your work on *Letters to Lucerne*. Good luck with it.

Next—thanks, Sparky for the valentine, it was appreciated so much; and, if you don't mind, I'll not throw it away. In fact, even if you do mind, I'll not throw it away. Also, you're right. I *did* notice the dress, and it *did* (and does) remind me of something—a very lovely evening and a high spot within a high spot as it were. We do have fun, don't we?

Carmen, thanks for offering me those fine books. And, yes, I'll take them very gladly. I have read a review of *For Whom the Bell Tolls* and it appealed to me very much. I saw the movie on *Kings Row*, and found it deeply stirring.

So you're under the impression you punctuate like a "drunken sailor," are you? Please allow me to straighten you out. You see, I happen to be on the censorship board and, consequently have to read hundreds of sailors' letters weekly; and I assure you, Madam, that even a sober sailor—we do have some, you know—can't even come close to you. In short, in case you haven't already gathered what I'm driving at, you're terrific!

Yes, the plans for Butch's and my N.Y. reunion are definite now except as to exact time and place. We shall definitely meet each other in the "big city" on Feb. 27th and 28th. I surely wish you could join us there, and I know we could depend on Butch for a vociferous "second" to that. Since you cannot be there, we will toast you and observe a short silence if you will promise not to be absent again.

As concerns my address, use New York until I give you another. I doubt very much that I'll be here when you come to New York, but we shall see. Stranger things have happened.

Now, as to why I hadn't written sooner. I have just completed a very lengthy and detailed inventory of all detachment property, preparing to signing for all of it. Enough of that.

Next, I married my roommate, Lt. Sam Porter of Boise, Idaho, off last Saturday afternoon. I was his best man, and the whole marriage went without a hitch.

Mother tells me she received a letter from you recently. She really enjoys your letters, as I can well understand.

Well, Carmen, guess I'll hit my sack, as it's nearly midnight.

Thanks again for everything, and good night. As ever, Harold. 1st Lt. H. L. Hiner, U.S.M.C. US.S. Boise, c/o Postmaster, New York City, New York

FEBRUARY 28,
POSTCARD FROM NEW YORK

Dear Sparky,

We made it. The Butcher and I are really having a great time. We drank a toast to you—and missed you. Here's Butch.

——Hi there, this is wonderful. *He's* as great as ever. We could use your charming company.

HAROLD & BUTCHER

MARCH 2, 1943. CENSORED

Dear Carmen,

This is only a short note to tell you how much I appreciated the books you sent. Both *Kings Row* and *Conrad Argosy.*

They are really fine, and—thanks so much. I have had no time to read them as yet, but so much the better, for I'll still have them left ahead of me when we go to sea.

Well, Sparky, by now I presume the card Butch and I sent from N.Y.C. has arrived. We surely had a great time. Just being with the Butcher-Boy is fun, and especially in such surroundings. We had plenty to talk over—must have sounded like a session of the sewing circle. We missed you. You let us down at a crucial moment, but all is forgiven.

How is your new play coming, Carmen, and when is it to be presented? I'll have to get the captain to ship me out for this performance if you can get me a ticket.

Also, what is the latest on the Wave situation? Be sure to keep me posted, for I'm deeply interested.

Well, Sparky, I'm going to sign off and turn in, for it's 1:30 and I'm dead tired. I'll write a longer letter very soon.

Have fun. As ever, Harold

MARCH 25, 1943. CENSORED

Dearest Carmen,

Please forgive me if you can for being so tardy in answering your last letter. Your books and pictures make me feel the more neglectful. Yes, they all arrived—all three books, the Omnibook and the pictures. Thank you so much for your thoughtfulness. As yet, I've had no time to read, but the time should come shortly.

Honestly, Sparky, for the last several weeks, we have been driving ourselves and our men literally night and day to get back into shape, and I am more than satisfied. I have a fine bunch of boys, and I'm sure they'll acquit themselves well.

As there is nothing I can tell you from here, I'll give you a brief account of the Kimball/Hiner reunion in New York, which, incidentally, came off in the nick of time. Yes, Sparky, you should really have been there. We would have had so much more fun. At any rate, I met the Butcher in Grand Central at 6:00 P.M., went to the hotel and cleaned up, and went out to a fine dinner. Later we went night-clubbing and sightseeing; and much later, after chewing over a considerable quantity of "fat," we turned in. The next morning, we had breakfast with Sam Forter (whose best man I was recently) and his wife and from there took the Staten Island Ferry trip so Butch could get a good look at the Statue of Liberty as well as the New York skyline. Then, after a little more craning of necks, we headed for the station to get Butch aboard his last train with about three minutes to spare. Gad, but it was great to talk to the Personality Kid again. Honestly, the trip would have been worth it for me even if I could have seen him for only an hour. He's really a fine fellow and one of my favorite friends.

Well, Carmen, as I said before, there really is nothing at this end to write about. However, I'll drop you a short note frequently. I'd suggest you send future mail to me Via V-mail.

Again, thanks so much for your thoughtfulness. Your books shall give me many happy hours. Goodnight, Carmen. Must turn in, for I'm due for about 4½ hours of sleep tonight—1½ hours now before I go on watch and 3 hours after I come off.

As ever, Harold   P.S. Would surely love to be back in the mountains to watch spring come. Must be heaven.

———— 🎵 ————

APRIL 1943

Dear Diary,

Well, the play is finally over. Everyone in class participated and loved it. I'm walking around with my head in the clouds. Last night was THE big night. We played to an overflow crowd and the applause was nonstop.

I wish Harold could have been here. I don't even know for sure where he is. The *Boise* is seaworthy again and is somewhere having "day practice" to check out their new guns before returning to the Pacific theater.

Art Culver is being persistent AND helpful. He did theatre work in college so was able to help me with the fight scene. He also helped the stage crew last night. Darn it, he hasn't forgotten I said I'd talk to Dad about the horses. I should have been honest and admitted I'd only choose to ride a horse if it were necessary to save my life. Now it's too late!.

Well, I guess it's put-up or shut-up time. Dad's bringing the horses in today. We had a long talk last night and he repeated all the things he's told me so many times before about horses.

"Now, Carmen, remember these are track horses. If one of them runs, the other one will think it's a race. I wouldn't get 'em above a trot if I were you. Hang on to the reins and if the horse gets too skittish, pull on 'em—but not too hard or she'll rear back and try to dump you. I'm taking it for granted Art knows what he's about."

"I'm sure he does, Dad. Now, don't you worry."

———— 🎵 ————

It was a beautiful day ... a bit crisp, but not cold. We mounted our horses and started up the street just four blocks to the edge of town on the south side. Six more blocks brought us by the college and to the lane leading to Aunt Alt's house. There were no houses on either side—we were really out in the country now. The horses were content with a fast walk, and I was beginning to feel relaxed enough to imitate some of the mannerisms I've seen my brother Dick use when he's showing off ... straight in the saddle, a smile on my face, elbows up, a light touch on the reins.

So far, I'd been leading the way, trying to cut a fine figure. Suddenly, I heard pounding hoofs as Art's horse caught up and passed me in a fast gallop. My horse lunged forward and took off at a dead run, and we quickly overtook Art's horse. I instinctively grabbed the saddle horn, which caused the reins to go slack in my hands. By the time I remembered to tighten my hold, my right foot slipped out of the stirrup and I lost my balance. I gritted my teeth, held on to the saddle horn, which no good horsewoman would ever think of doing, until I managed to get my foot back in the stirrup. I was so scared I considered bailing out, but didn't have the nerve to do it. My fanny was bouncing sky high above the saddle, and I realized how totally ridiculous I looked and knew I'd not a shred of dignity left.

I could hear Art's horse in back of me, and we were running a race both horses wanted to win. If I had let go of the saddle horn long enough to tighten the reins, I probably would have bounced right off the horse's back. Instead, I tightened my knees and lower legs as much as I could to minimize the bouncing, then pulled hard on the reins. FINALLY ... my horse responded.

Art caught up, and I realized he'd been struggling to rein in his horse ... he was gasping for breath, and the look on his face told me this hadn't been his idea of a joyride.

"Ye gods! I've never been on a horse like this one before!" When he caught his breath, and my heart stopped pounding, we turned around and started toward town. I worried that as soon as the horses realized they were headed for home they'd start to run again. Thankfully, they'd had their run and leisurely walked us home.

"Carmen, I never dreamed I'd ever be on a horse, running down a country lane, with a beautiful girl who rides like the wind. *I'll never forget this day!*"

Neither will I, nor will I EVER repeat it, I promised myself.

Thank goodness he was so busy holding on, he didn't have time to look at me. What the heck—what he doesn't know won't hurt him.

I've decided. I'm not going to join the Waves ... my brothers and parents are too much against it. Leora Petty, whom I've known all my life and who teaches Physical Ed., feels the same way I do. We flipped a coin to decide whether to look for a job in Los Angeles or Denver, and it came up L.A.

Our school salary is paid on a 12-month basis, so we'll have income during the summer. Not much, but enough to tide us over while we look into possibilities in Los Angeles. Leora would like to be an airline stewardess. That sounds okay to me. We hear it pays well.

APRIL 18, 1943, CENSORED
AT SEA

Dear Carmen,

Just another of my short notes in answer to your sweet letters. Have received your V-Mail letters of April 7 and 11. Thank you so much for them. Will you please send me Butch's Jacksonville, Fla. address, as I owe him a letter and do not have his new address.

Well, for once, I do have one bit of news from this end. Surprise, huh? At any rate, I made Captain several days ago. Am quite happy about it, as you may imagine, for that quite definitely puts me out of the junior officer class.

Have heard from both Harriet and Jim recently. Harriet and her husband are having a wonderful time in Phoenix, while Jim recently became the proud possessor, as he puts it, of "1-A" status. This last is not for publication, as I'm not sure Mother knows it yet. I don't know when he'll be called, but I hope it will not be very soon.

Nothing more to say, so guess I'll knock off. My regards to all our friends, and I'll write again when I have the time.

As ever, Harold

Dear Diary,

It's obvious the *Boise* is about to sail again, and I'm sure it won't be to a resort area. The signals are all there ... send V Mail ... he's been working night and day and feels his boys will acquit themselves well ... there will be time to read.

I don't like it when he tells me to have fun. Is he trying to spare me by making light of his leaving, or is he hoping I'll find someone else and leave him alone? I guess I feel this way when I think about him going into combat again. I think I'd feel better if he'd complain and say he wishes he didn't have to go ... but that will never happen ... Marines don't complain, "they tell the truth, do their best no matter how trivial the task, choose the difficult right over the easy wrong, never whine or make excuses, look out for the group before they look out for themselves." Good thing I'm not a marine!

High School Play To Be Presented

Miss Carmen Leigh of the Cedar City High School Dramatic department announces that the school play "Letters to Lucerne" is to be presented this Friday, March 19th, in the public school auditorium. The curtain will go up promptly at 8:15 p.m., admission will be 30¢ as announced before. Tickets will be available at the High school during school hours, but since a large crowd is anticipated tickets will be sold at the door also.

Many New York newspapers have reviewed "Letters to Lucerne" as a truly great play. Huge audiences attended this show at the various theatres in New York and vicinity, and have been profuse in their praise of the authors, Fritz Rotter, and Allen Vincent. Of it, the New York Daily News said, "Letters to Lucerne," a human and moving drama of the war. This, I think, is the first of the newer war dramas to command serious attention—it was completely holding with last night's audience." The New York Journal-America had this to say: "Now this is, let us admit, a poignant situation, full of heartbreak if not tragedy. This is a noble argument."

The Cedar City High School feels it a great privilege to present a play of such prominence. Students expected to turn in a really fine performance are Adele Sevy as the German girl; Idonna Gower as the schoolmistress; and Erwin Heaps who plays the part of the Handsome German boy. These students along with the other members of the cast will do their utmost to bring this play to you vividly and interestingly. We urge you to be with us Friday night and enjoy the telling of this really beautiful story.

Carmen (above) *and her Los Angeles roommate Leora.*

CHAPTER 6

More Combat

JUNE 1943

The *Boise* departs the States on June 8, 1943, pointing her bow eastward, sailing with a convoy to the Mediterranean. This time she sets sail without Capt. Mike Moran, who has been elevated to a position of greater responsibility.

Back in the groove; day after day of Condition 2 watches—four hours on and four hours off. All division duties, extra duties, and sleep have to be caught up in the four hours off between regular watches. Capt. Harold Hiner, now commanding officer of the marine detachment, is ship's service officer, laundry officer, barbershop officer (featuring 15¢ haircuts), recorder of a summary court martial, and officer of turret three in the main battery.

Harold loves the sea almost as much as he loves the mountains. He never tires of the flying fish, porpoises, whales, albatross, and other sea birds; the royal blue of the water and the foaming white wake in the daytime. Then at night, the soft moon and the phosphorescence left in the ship's wake as it runs its zigzag pattern to elude submarines.

As the ship passes Gibraltar on a quiet night, Captain Hiner is on the bridge with the new skipper, Capt. Hewitt Thebeaud. The only static on that beautiful evening comes from radar plot. The officer in charge of radar has very recently joined the ship and obviously feels that the skipper does not appreciate the gravity of the situation. He communicates his

71

thoughts in person by arriving on the bridge in a helmet and wearing two life jackets, one kapok and one inflatable. The new skipper proves himself to be very decisive, for that "newly arrived" officer is "newly departed" as soon as the ship reaches Algiers.

JUNE 10, 1943. AT SEA. CENSORED

Dear Sparky,

Should be dropping mail soon now, so here's a letter in answer to your last two—and the card.

Thanks a hundred for the Bryce Canyon card, Carmen. I've never in my life been homesick in the common sense, but I do miss that wonderful inter-mountain country. I love the sea, but it could never have the appeal for me the mountains have. If anything ever causes me to leave the Marine Corps, it will be the call of the open mountain life.

At the present, I'm not sure as to how things stand with Jim and my brother-in-law, as I have not heard from them for some time. (Incidentally, the last letter I have from you is dated May 23rd.) I hope, however, and presume, their status is unchanged.

Don't worry, I have not forgotten the rain checks either, for I hold the other halves, and I hope to collect them some day in the not too distant future.

Well, Carmen, as was the case last summer, I have nothing I can talk about except what I find in your letters, so keep me posted. If you're still in Cedar City, please give my regards to your family.

Good-bye for now, Sparky. Have fun and take care of yourself. Love, Harold.   Capt. H. L. Hiner USMC

Dear Diary,

I'm glad I got Harold's letter before Leora and I leave. It's a bit scary, thinking about going to a place where I don't know anyone, but I'm not going to mention this to Mother ... she's upset enough. Leora's brother loaned us his car and both families gave us gas stamps. She'll drive, thank goodness. I've never driven a car except around Cedar City.

Leora has an aunt in Van Nuys, and she's invited us to stay with her for a few days while we look for an apartment. We're leaving as soon as we finish closing out the teaching year and get packed. Mother cries every time she looks at me. I feel like a heel.

The cadet class has finished pre-flight and is being sent somewhere in California for flight training. It's just as well. Art Culver is a really nice guy and I like him, but he's getting a lot more serious than I want to be. It's the usual thing and understandable. These guys know they are going into combat and that makes them more sentimental. I promised to write, but who knows ... I'll probably never see him again.

JUNE 20, 1943

We're on our way! The folks wave good-bye from the porch and Mother is crying something awful. Good grief ... you'd think I was ten years old.

Every time we stop for gas, we have to put oil in the car. I didn't know you had to do that ... this is costing a bundle. Finally, we get to Leora's aunt's. She's nice and California is beautiful—lots of green grass, colorful flowers, and huge palm trees. Tomorrow is apartment-hunting day.

JUNE 21, 1943

Leora's uncle suggested we check out some apartments he's noticed on east Westmoreland Street. It's a nice area, not far from downtown Los Angeles. Can you believe our luck ... one apartment has been vacated and the landlady, after putting us through the third degree, agreed to rent it to us.

It's a small efficiency apartment. One large room with a pull-down bed, a bath, and a pullman kitchen. It's not roomy, but the closet is large enough for two and we think we can get along with a small kitchen, since neither of us is much interested in cooking anyway. It's a cinch we can't afford a large apartment in this fancy area. The apartments are built around a courtyard, beautifully landscaped, and only a block from a downtown streetcar stop.

JUNE 23, 1943

Have already found we can cook an entire meal on a two-burner. We lost no time interviewing with the airlines. Leora qualified easily. I, it turns out, am too tall ... at 5'7½" I'm above the maximum height for a stewardess. I want Leora to do what she wants, though I'm concerned our apartment arrangement will be jeopardized ... she decided against it.

We applied to the Bank of America, which is now hiring women because of the scarcity of men. Good thing we have college degrees because, though it isn't required of men, it is of women. I will be at the 7th and Olive branch and Leora at 7th and Spring. That is if, in the next two weeks, we can learn the NCR machine the tellers are required to know.

We've been in our apartment one week and have already met several of our new neighbors. Irys Hedman is married to an army sergeant who is presently overseas. She works as a book-keeper for Rhodes Jewelers on Broadway. Lee Kirby has an apartment like ours. We wonder how she can afford it on her salary until she candidly confesses that her boss is paying the rent. Then there's "Doc." I call him "Old Doc" because he's in his late thirties and that seems old to me. He's a bachelor and definitely on the prowl. He seems nice enough as a neighbor, but I have no intention of being alone with him ... *EVER*! He has all the moves and his favorite philosophy is, "it never hurts to try," and, when his advances fail, " you can take the girl out of the country, but you can't take the country out of the girl."

JULY 6, 1943. AT SEA. V MAIL. CENSORED

Dear Sparky,

How goes everything there by now? Where are you now, and what are you doing? What is all the latest?

How is that for a start? You see, we haven't received any mail now, for almost six weeks, so I'm really stale on what has been happening. Should hit the jackpot, however, when it starts to catch up, so it won't be so bad. You can always count on the old Law of Compensation.

As usual, of course, I can tell you nothing of the interesting things we are seeing and doing, but you must be used to these empty letters of mine by now.

I'm about to get back into shape. The soft "shore" life we were leading for a while almost spoiled us, but I'm practically healthy again. Have acquired by far the best tan I have ever had and have had my hair cut off to about three-quarters of an inch. I feel great! Don't look too sharp, I suppose, but looks don't make much difference back here.

Haven't heard from Jim for almost two months now, so I'm not sure of his status at present. Surely hope he is still in San Diego. Haven't heard from Harriet for a like period of time, and it's quite likely her husband has been ordered out, too.

Well, Carmen, this looks like a terribly short letter and is— but I must close if I'm to get this into the mail on time. More than that, I have nothing more to say anyway. If I received a letter from the other end like this, I wouldn't like it a little bit, but we are so restricted that all our letters accomplish is to let those back home know that as of such and such a date, we out here are well and happy.

Take care of yourself, Carmen. Have fun. Be seein' you, Harold L. Hiner, Capt. H. L. Hiner U.S.M.C.

The *Boise* reaches Oran, Algiers, June 21, 1932, where she joins the U.S. 8th fleet and reports for duty in Task Force 81 under the command of Rear Adm. John L. Hall, USN. He addresses the following message to *Boise*: "AMPHINAW PROUDLY WELCOMES CAPTAIN, OFFICERS AND CREW OF SHIP ALREADY FOUND STRONG IN BATTLE." The *Boise* ties up alongside the KG5, and the *Admiral Howe* and her marines practice shooting alongside the Algerian Royal Marines at Maison Blanc.

At Malta and other African ports, there are 3,266 ships, ranging from battleships to motor torpedo boats, manned by more than 80,000 officers and men. They are preparing to take part in the biggest single fleet movement in naval history. Not only are they from the British and American navies, but from the Royal Canadian, Royal Indian, Dutch, Polish, and Greek navies as well. Within forty-eight hours after the landing of the first load of troops, the entire fleet of landing vessels will make another round trip to Africa and return to Sicily loaded with men and supplies.

During the days preceding the invasion of Sicily, the ships make dummy runs, and all hands are urged to do a lot of sunbathing. In port there are movies every night, record concerts, and occasional swimming parties held off the port side. This activity is deliberate and is a ploy designed to fool the enemy so that they will not suspect invasion is imminent.

The men of the *Boise* are ready. Gunnery practice is given top priority, and every inch of space available is made ready to carry men and equipment. It is the eve of the invasion, and all hands are watching the activity on the airstrip. Huge transport planes are surrounded by the paratroopers who will be landed far behind the enemy lines before zero hour. A year of concentrated training is behind them. Their mission is to take and hold the enemy positions until the seaborne land forces arrive to relieve them.

The paratroopers memorize their cloth maps and orders, check and pack their gear . . . each of the many pockets in their jumping suits is crammed full. The jumping boots, trademark of their profession, are laced with extra tightness. There is no horseplay, no heroics, no boasts, and no doubts.

The colonel, tallest of all, gives his final instructions, ending with the password, and adds: "You'd better get it right, because there will be itchy trigger fingers." Time for takeoff is set for 2055. The men have a few minutes left for a smoke, a drink of water, and a little talk. They take the last puff, tighten the chin straps on their helmets, and climb aboard. One by one, they disappear into their planes. The commander salutes the assembled group, then he, too, disappears into a plane.

The liberation of Europe has begun, and the second front

is about to be opened. Zero hour is 0243, tomorrow, July 10, 1943.

By evening, the *Boise*'s convoy is at sea. At dawn the next morning, Captain Hiner reports topside and sees ships of all sizes and kinds, in all directions as far as the eye can see. He enters his turret, number three, and prepares his men for the coming battle. The sea is choppy, and some of the smaller craft look more like submarines than surface craft. The much-rumored air umbrella turns out to be an occasional group of Spitfires. Somebody wisecracks that it's like the naked emperor's new clothes—"only the good people can see them." Morale is improved, however, when a large flight of bombers flies over on its way to lay some eggs on *Il Duce*.

In a few hours, the paratroopers have landed and are doing the job expected of them. Shore batteries are firing on the Allies' naval convoys, the transports are lowering their landing barges, and the small crafts are beginning to move slowly toward the beach. The landing boats work like ants between the ships and the shore, loaded with the men who will have to storm the beaches.

There are no Allied airfields close by as yet. This is enemy territory, and the Axis forces are throwing all kinds of planes at us. Messerschmitts roar down through the canyons under radar and hit an ammunition ship alongside the *Boise*. Another ship beside her wanders into the minefield, and the headset phones record the plaintive cry: "Shady is caught in the alligator." The *Boise* is a lucky ship.

So far the guns on our ships have been effective against shore batteries. Each time they turn on the searchlights to pick out target, a few well-placed salvos erupt from our ships and the lights go out and stay out.

It's daylight now, and our troops have landed. The Germans retreat long enough to allow them to come ashore so they can pull another Dunkirk, then start to advance again. This time the Germans are caught off guard. The *Boise* and other ships, chosen for their expert gunnery, have spotters on the beach to pick out targets and give their range. On receiving word, the tanks are moving in; they fire a barrage that completely demolishes the Goering tank division, comprised of Mark IV tanks. Of the 1,600 men in the tank division, only 22 are saved.

The Germans can't believe that their strategy has failed. Knowing ground troops don't have equipment to cope with tanks the size of the Mark IV, they had expected an easy slaughter of the Allied troops. Never before in the history of warfare had ships been able to fire on tanks in support of ground troops. The new radar on the *Boise* and others of the newer ships have proved their worth. General Patton himself praises the *Boise* for its excellent gunnery.

AUGUST 8, 1943. AT SEA. CENSORED

Dear Sparky,

The last four days have been wonderful days, for they brought our first mail since we left the States around the first of June. Carmen, I doubt you could possibly realize what it is like to get mail from "home" after so long a time, way out here where there is – – – – (slipped). I had ten letters from you, and I have read each of them about four times. Happy days!

I suppose by now you are back in L.A. on your new job. How do you like it by now? I'll bet—and I hope—you are really enjoying it. I think it is a good thing for you to get away from Cedar and schoolteaching for the summer at least. Tell me something of your job, where you are living, and all the rest.

So glad to hear about your brothers. It's great you could get home to see them. When is Ham to be married? Haven't seen my brother and sister together since Sept. of '41, and haven't seen either of them since April of '42. Surely would love to see them.

Gad, Sparky, but I got a shock yesterday when I received a letter from Father, written on July 18, to the effect that Jim was to be married on July 22. Gave my stomach the jumps. I know now why mothers cry at weddings. I guess I have a brand new sister-in-law by now if everything went according to plan. I hope my parents were able to attend the wedding, for I'd hate to have my little brother get married all "alone."

Well, Sparky, censorship regulations have been relaxed a bit on the immediate campaign. We may now tell you that we are in the Mediterranean and we participated in the invasion of Sicily. Our mission was to act as naval fire support for the first waves of landing troops. We were subjected to our first aerial bombings, and we came through unscathed. The fire from our main battery was accurate and telling, and we were later commended by the army and by our task force leader. I would not have missed this opening of the "second front" for anything. It was a well-planned operation, and was very well executed. There were several ticklish periods, but on the whole, there weren't so many thrills as in the Pacific.

The travel posters aren't far off in their claims for a cruise in the Mediterranean. It is absolutely beautiful over here. The water is a vivid blue, and the islands we see are rugged and picturesque. The climate (for the present) is hot and dry, with cool nights. The North African cities are extremely colorful and intriguing, being at the same time unbelievably and unutterably filthy! Honestly, the filth is monstrous. The largest cities have little or no sanitary measures such as sewage systems. Moslems abound, of course, and on liberty, one sees every possible Allied uniform. It is the most heterogeneous mass of humanity and civilization I have ever seen, and I don't know where it is duplicated.

Well, I guess that's about all the news from this end for now. Keep me posted, and I, in turn, will try to write more frequently. Thanks a million for your letters.

As ever, Harold   Capt. H. L. Hiner, USMC

SEPTEMBER 5 TO 19, 1943

The surrender of Italy is imminent, and it is important to seize and occupy the city of Taranto and the naval base in order to deny it to the Germans. On September 8 the *Boise* sails from Algiers carrying 788 officers and men of the British 1st Airborne Division with equipment—jeeps, motorcycles, light field pieces, and bicycles. They rendezvous northeast of Malta with the heavyweights of the British navy—HMS *Howe*, HMS *King George*, and six destroyers.

The *Boise* is the only American ship to participate with the British fleet in accepting the surrender of the Italian fleet as it leaves Taranto. The British give the *Boise* the dubious honor of leading the fleet into the mined harbor. Since *Boise* has neither pilots nor line-handling details, the marine detachment, under Captain Hiner's command, is put over the side with Tommy guns to act in that capacity. It is likely this will be the only time a capital ship will be tied up in wartime by a marine detachment.

The Italian fleet steams out of the harbor as the Allies put in and are overflown by a JU52 carrying the German general staff, departing at that late hour. The Germans arrogantly shower the fleet with every recognition signal in the book. When the *Boise* pulls into Malta two days later the proud Italian fleet lies in a shambles, having been pulverized by the Luftwaffe for their defection.

As some of the newly landed troops make their way inland, the first sign of civilization they see is a large vineyard. The farmer isn't carrying a gun, so the soldiers approach him and, in their best Brooklyn Italian, talk to him. He replies in the best of English, "Hiya, kids."

It so happens he lived in Hackensack, New Jersey, for eighteen years and ran a press shop there. He is happy to see the Americans take over. "Damn right," he said. "*Fascisti* is no good. No movies here. In America I was treated okay and there are movies on every corner. Here they take everything. Now I have nothing." He is determined to treat the Americans okay, so he passes around what little wine he has.

After reaching Gela, the troops move on to Comiso and fight their way to the airport. Once the airport is secured by the Allies, the Second Front is opened and will go down in history as a turning point in the war.

U.S.S. BOISE

July 15, 1943

NOTICE FOR: ALL HANDS

The following messages concerning the parts played by the U.S.S. BOISE in connection with the landing of troops on the island of Sicily are being published for information

---

FROM: CTF 81

TO: BOISE   July 12, 1943

Report with vessels your command to CTF 81 in Biscayne. Continue present duties until directed otherwise. WELL DONE.

FROM: CTF 81   July 12, 1943

TO: BOISE

The magnificent support of your groups contributed greatly to success WELL DONE. Pass to SAVANNAH and destroyers concerned.

Message received from Admiral Hall (CTF 81) to Captain Thebeaud just prior to his departure.

July 13, 1943

"See you soon. Best of luck. *Thanks for outstanding support.*"

FROM: SAVANNAH   July 15, 1943

TO: BOISE

Captain: Naval Liaison Officers we have aboard say that you knocked out some tanks of the German Goering Division. They also say that Boise fire support was super excellent throughout. My hearty congratulations. Hope we both get a chance at some ships too. CARY

FROM: Com EIGHTH FLEET   July 15, 1943

TO: ALL HANDS WEST TASKFORCE

Due to careful planning, excellent seamanship, gunnery and engineering and a high standard of proficiency and devotion to duty by all hands the most difficult and complicated task of landing our troops on hostile shores has been successfully accomplished. Informed reports of specially meritorious acts and accomplishments have been many. I consider that all from the Force Commanders to the lowest ratings have performed splendidly and are deserving of the highest praise. WELL DONE. It is now our duty to support and maintain and build up the forces which have been landed. Carry on. Task Force and Task Group Commanders pass to non holders this system your command.

B.K. CULVER,
Commandeer, U.S. Navy,
Executive Officer

U.S.S. BOISE

SEPTEMBER 20, 1943

MEMORANDUM FOR: All Division officers.

The following will be published at quarters today:

1. Liberty will be granted as follows:

    Men 1300 to 1900

    Officers 1300 to 2030

    (One section will be granted liberty each day).

2. Liberty uniform:

    Officers and C.P.O.'s: Khaki with black tie (blouses optional) cap or garrison cap. White uniform optional.

    Enlisted men: Undress whites with neckerchief and white caps.

3. Looting, which is the taking of private property without permission, is a military crime and will not be tolerated. Enemy fire-arms or other property will not be taken as souvenirs, but will be turned over to the army authorities.

4. All ships or craft sending Liberty parties ashore will supply shore patrols in the proportion of one patrolman for each 20 men on liberty and one officer for each 5 men on patrol. The boat landing for liberty parties is located at the bulkhead between Piers #4 and #5.

5. The uniform for Shore Patrol is undress whites, neckerchief, white hat, leggings, belt and pistol, brassard, and nightstick. Shore Patrol report to the Senior Shore Patrol Officer, 95 Via Emerico Amari, for instructions at 1230.

6. *BARS AND RESTAURANTS.* Intoxicating beverages will be purchased only in establishments authorized by the Provost Marshall and placarded as such. Under no circumstances will intoxicating beverages be carried or consumed on the streets or at any unauthorized place. The same, found in possession of personnel under the aforementioned circumstances shall be confiscated and destroyed.

7. Circulation of United States money ashore is prohibited. You *MUST HAVE* INVASION MONEY, OBTAINABLE at the rate of 100 liras for $1.00.

8. Church Services are as follows:

    Catholic—Chaplain R.F. McManus, Lieutenant, USNR,

Mass at 0730 in the N.O.B. Chapel. Confessions at 1800 at the Chaplain's office at the Naval Operating Base.

Protestant—Chaplain I.V. Ellis, Lieutenant, USNR Sunday Services at 0900 at H.E.C.P. Rec. Room, also at 1000 in N.O.B. Chapel.

The Army also has Catholic, Protestant and Jewish services in town.

Recreation: Red Cross Movie Theatre Piazza Guiseppe Verdi beside the Court House. Movies at 1800 and 2000 daily except Fridays; reservations through the Army Special Service, 7th Army Headquarters, Via Roma.

9. Venereal disease in this area is known to be prevalent. Eight of ten (80%) prostitutes recently examined showed evidence of active infectious venereal disease.

Attention is called to all personnel to keep fit for the job at hand by avoiding exposure to venereal disease. When exposure occurs secure prompt prophylaxis at any of the following locations:

(a) Army Dispensary Via Coura (next to the Bank of Italy).

(b) At Port Sick Call—across the street from headquarters.

(c) U.S. Naval Dispensary—Via Liberta and Via Florestano Pepe.

(d) U.S. Naval Shore Patrol Headquarters—95 Via Americo Amare.

(e) N.O.B. Barracks (Hotel Igeia).

B.K. CULVER
COMMANDER, U.S. NAVY,

The following excerpts are quoted from the Suva Master-Directive for all officers:

CURFEW. Both military and civil laws prohibit any person, except when on official business or with a curfew pass, to be out of doors in the Suva area between the hours 2330–0500. Violators are subject to arrest and punishment by fine or imprisonment—or both.

HOTEL. Grand Pacific. Victoria Parade, opposite Albert Park. Tel. 287. (1) Meals: breakfast, 0730, price 75¢; lunch 1300, price $1; dinner, 1830, price $1.12. Variety of drinks available. (2) Standard price for rooms $3.75 per day, including meals. (3) Bar open until 1800. NOTE: Advisable to make reservations for meals in advance.

LIQUOR LAWS: No liquor is to be given to Fijians or Indians. A hotel lodger may not give liquor to anyone after the bar is closed who is not a lodger in the same hotel.

NATIVES, Conduct Toward. It is forbidden: to fraternize with natives; drive in vehicles in company with them; dance with them; engage in sports against them; supply liquor to them; enter Kava saloons; enter native villages except on military duty or in company with organized sight-seeing parties; enter native dwellings, social halls or place of entertainment; consort with native women. "Native" includes Fijians and Indians.

OUT-OF-BOUNDS AREAS: All ordnance buildings, storage and warehouses, pump houses, and electrical supply installations are out-of-bounds except to those required on duty.

RESTAURANTS: Local food supply limited; not recommended. Arrangements should be made to mess liberty parties and shore patrols aboard if possible. Certain restaurants and ice cream parlors have had ice cream and sodas approved by the Force Surgeon, such places identified by conspicuous sign in red and white reading: "APPROVED BY ARMY INSPECTOR." Places not showing this sign are out-of-bounds to military personnel.

U.S.S. Boise

ASIATIC-PACIFIC THEATER
AUGUST 5, 1942 to SEPTEMBER 15, 1944

Aug. 5, 1942	Lone Tokyo Raid
Sept. 27, 1942	Guadalcanal
Oct. 11-12, 1942	Battle of Cape Esperance
Jan. 25-26, 1944	Aleishafen, New Guinea
April 22, 1944	Humboldt Bay, Dutch New Guinea
April 29-30, 1944	Sawar & Wakde Airdromes, Dutch New Guinea
May 17, 1944	Wakde-Toem Area, Dutch New Guinea
May 27, 1944	Biak Island
July 2, 1944	Noemfoor Island
July 30, 1944	Cape Sansapao, New Guinea
Sept. 15, 1944	Halmahera Islands

* Harold Hiner was aboard.

FLAGSHIP
Commander in Chief – Southwest Pacific Area
General of the Army – Douglas Mac Arthur
January 4-13, 1945 – June 3-15, 1945

EUROPEAN THEATER
JULY 10, 1943, TO SEPTEMBER 16, 1943

July 10-14, 1943	Gela, Sicily
Aug. 12-14, 1943	Cape Calava & Cape Milazzo, Sicily
Aug. 17, 1943	Palmi, Italy
Sept. 9, 1943	Taranto, Italy
Sept. 12-16, 1943	Salerno, Italy

PHILIPPINE–BORNEO OPERATIONS
OCTOBER 20, 1944 TO JUNE 11, 1945

Oct. 20-24, 1944	San Pedro Bay, Leyte Gulf
Oct. 25, 1944	Battle of Surigao Straits
Nov. 1, 1944	Heavy Air Attacks, Leyte Gulf
Dec. 15, 1944	San Jose, Mindoro
Jan. 9-14, 1945	Lingayen Gulf, Luzon
Feb. 13-17, 1945	Corregidor and Bataan Peninsula, Luzon
Mar. 8-12, 1945	Zamboanga, Mindanao
May 1-3, 1945	Tarakan, Borneo
June 8-11, 1945	Brunei Bay, Borneo

NIGHT SURFACE ENGAGEMENTS

Battle of Cape Esperance	Oct. 11-12, 1942
Battle of Surigao Straits	Oct. 25, 1944

*

Boise in combat, in the Mediterranean.

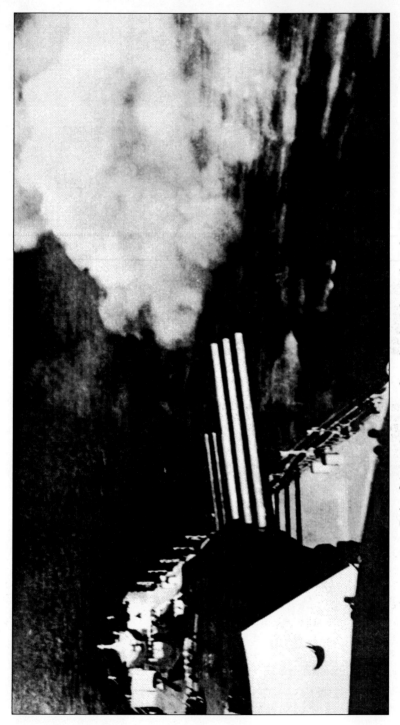

Boise firing at German tanks on beach, Gela, Sicily, July 1943.

Boise *recovering aircraft in battle, Gela, Sicily, July 11, 1943.*

CHAPTER 7

Life in the Big City

———🎺———

Dear Diary,

Living in a big city is a lot different than living in a small town where you know and can trust everyone. I don't admit it to my folks, but I get lonesome sometimes and feel kind of lost. I used to feel like a big fish in a little pond. Now I feel totally obscure and unimportant.

I haven't heard from Harold since August. He was in the Mediterranean then, but the war there is mostly inland now, so I imagine the *Boise* has been sent elsewhere.

A lot of people, especially servicemen, pass through L.A. on the way to someplace else. Mother says several of my old boyfriends have called recently to find out where I am and have said they will probably be in L.A. sometime soon. Karl Burgess, who used to live with us and is like a brother, called, and we went to dinner and had a great visit. Phillip Stuart, the night clerk I dated the summer I worked in Zion, also called recently. He's with the Merchant Marines and stationed near here. I went to dinner with him but spent most of the evening fighting him off, so that's the end of that. It's just my bad luck the guy I'd love to see is on a ship berthed on the East Coast when it's stateside.

I do like my job and our apartment, and I've made friends with some girls at work and some who live in our complex. We go to restaurants after work and quite often on Sundays to "Tea Dances" at the Ambassador or Biltmore hotels. Servicemen are bused in from bases, and the banks and other businesses encourage their single women employees to attend and dance with them.

Our neighbor, "Old Doc," has a car, and he takes us to the beach and other places we might not otherwise get to since none of us has a car ... and couldn't get gas if we did. As long as we make sure we aren't EVER alone with him, he's fun, and I think he enjoys playing the big shot.

Leora, with her black hair and eyes, and voluptuous figure, attracts a lot of attention. One night recently, we came home on the bus, and she chatted all the way to our stop with a young army captain just home from combat in the Pacific. The captain got off when we did, though we knew it wasn't his original destination. We had to walk a block on an unlighted street to reach our apartment, and I could see that Leora was beginning to realize, as I did, how vulnerable we were. I secreted the front door key out of my purse and held it in my hand. I took her hand in mine so she could feel the key, hoping she would get the message ... she did.

At our front door, we said good-bye to the captain, hoping he would be reasonable, but he was furious when we refused to invite him in. While Leora distracted him, I got the key in the lock and we slipped inside. He obviously had a bad case of war nerves or battle fatigue, because he went crazy ... yelled and pounded on the door until Old Doc upstairs called the police.

They discovered he was carrying a gun.

After the police took him away, I called Doc and thanked him. His reply was typical for him: "You're welcome. If anyone's going to seduce you, I'd rather it'd be me." Leora promised never again to talk to strangers.

Leora and I get along well most of the time, except she's not as particular as I am about the apartment housekeeping. It's so small, I like to keep it neat and uncluttered. When I left for work this morning, she was still in bed and had called in sick. I just got home, and she is gone and the place looks like a cyclone struck it. The wall bed is still down and unmade, and her clothes and jewelry scattered everywhere. I guess she either felt better and decided to go to work or has gone to her aunt's, which she often does for the weekend. Obviously, she left in a hurry, and I can't find a note or any clue to her whereabouts. She'll call later, but in the meantime I'm furious.

I made the bed, sat down on it to drink a cup of coffee, feeling lonely and frustrated, and now the darn doorbell's ringing. Please God, don't let it be Doc ... I don't want to deal with him right now, especially when I'm here alone.

I considered not answering the door, but curiosity got the better of me. I'm glad ... it's Art Culver, looking squared away and handsome in his air force uniform, with the gold bar of 2nd Lieutenant on his shoulder. I'm glad to see him even though I'm embarrassed I didn't answer his last letter and let him know where to find me. I knew his base was nearby, but assumed, since he is from Arcadia and knows lots of girls in this area, he wouldn't be interested in me.

"Carmen, you look wonderful. I apologize for showing up like this. We just got word we're being shipped out, so I called your mother and got your address. I phoned here, but there was no answer. I have only a few hours before I have to be back on base ... we're leaving tomorrow. I couldn't leave without seeing you."

I feel flustered. I want to tell him how glad I am to see him, which I am, but don't want to lead him on ... I'm embarrassed because the apartment is a mess. I can tell he wants to kiss me and I sort of want him to, but then I don't. Besides, I'm alone here and he's going overseas ... I know how that makes the guys feel. His eyes compel me to look at him, and suddenly I realize how vulnerable I feel, and how weary I am of all the good-byes and the sad eyes in the faces of guys I know and care about.

"Sorry, there's no place to sit down," I apologize. "My roommate left the bed this way. If you'll help me put it up we'll be able to find the chairs."

"Carmen," he took hold of my arms and looked square at me. "I didn't think we'd be flying out this soon. I really care for you. Is there any chance we can leave the bed down for a while?"

"I ..." I can't believe I'm hesitating and almost want to say yes. I care for him, though not in the same way I do Harold ... after all, Harold and I have a long history. But I like him a lot and I feel lonely and sad for all of us who are living through this nightmare.

"I'm sorry, Art, I ... I can't."

"I shouldn't have asked." He put the bed in the wall. "Hey, what do you say we go out for dinner? I know a great place, good food and dancing! Sorry, my dear, there's no chance for a horseback ride on such short notice," he grinned at me, then turned serious. "I warn you, when I get back I'll try again, only then I'll go about it the right way."

He's driving a car, and the "place" is a nightclub filled with GIs and their girls. I'm sure the food is good, but I'd rather dance. The music is all my favorites ... "In the Mood," "Pennsylvania 6500," "Tangerine," "Sentimental Journey," "Let's Fall in Love." It's the most fun I've had for ages. Unfortunately we had to leave early so he can get to the base on time.

Back at the apartment, he gave me an early Christmas card. A picture of him by his plane, a P38 fighter, alongside a small decorated Christmas tree. Then a lingering good-bye kiss and the inevitable question: Carmen, will you write to me?

I didn't have the heart to say no. Why not? He's a friend.

Following the surrender of Italy, the fighting has swung inland, so cruiser fire support is no longer required. On September 19, 1943, the *Boise* sails to Palermo to await further orders. There, she is released from duty with the Eighth Fleet and ordered to return to the States for reassignment, arriving in New York on November 15, 1943.

The *Boise* and her crew have an eighteen-day availability at the Brooklyn Navy Yard. While there, the men are given short liberty in New York and are able to telephone family and friends.

On December 6, 1943, *Boise* sets sail, heading south. She arrives at the Panama Canal Zone on the 10th and reports to Commander Seventh Fleet Adm. T. C. Kincaid, and on the 12th departs for Milne Bay, New Guinea.

The *Boise* then serves with the Seventh Fleet units engaged in the occupation and consolidation of Eastern New Guinea. In January 1944 she operates in the Buna area, where she engages in a bombardment of the Madang–Alexishafen area, then returns to Milne Bay to base and train for forthcoming operations.

Dear Diary,

I'm thrilled to talk to Harold. His letters are great, but to hear his voice is the best. He sounds fine, but wishes they could be stateside longer. He knows people in the New York area—he's dated there before, so I'm sure he'll have a good time. I'll admit I'm jealous and wish he'd be on the West Coast for a change.

I'm beginning to think every guy I know, except Harold, gets to L.A. at some time or another. Just this week, Eccles Caine showed up at the bank. I was busy with a long line at my window, so didn't notice he was there. When he got to the head of the line, I was clearing the N.C.R. and didn't look up until I heard a familiar voice, "How are you, Charmin' Carmen?"

There he was, one of my best friends from college. In uniform, of course, obviously pleased to have surprised me. He is en route to his base and can't stay over, but wanted to ask if I'd come to Logan for the Holiday Ball. He'll be on leave then and wants me to stay with his family.

"I'll come if I can get transportation and time off," I promised.

"Leave it to me, I'll get you there." We had loads of fun and saw a few of our old friends. Unfortunately, he was hoping for a commitment of some kind. I should have known.

Why is it that with all the good men I know, I can't get over the one I never get to see? I can see what's going to happen to me. I'm going to be left on the family tree. There I'll be ... dried-up and old, swinging in the breeze, the only old maid in an enormous, prolific family. In Cedar City, girls are expected to marry when they graduate from high school. If you go to college it's okay, but you're a reject if, when you finish, you don't marry immediately.

FEBRUARY 17, 1944. AT SEA. CENSORED

Dearest Carmen,

I received your valentine on the 13th, which is pretty terrific timing! How do you do it? I really appreciate it. Also received that Christmas cake from your mother the same day. Guess it had followed us from the Mediterranean, for all the wrapping was torn off. Consequently, I didn't know your mother's initials, and when I wrote her tonight, I had to address her letter simply "Mrs. Leigh." Cake came through in good shape.

Thank you, Carmen, for the Colliers. I do like it! Again you've shown me you are the most thoughtful person I know.

Right now it's 3:30 in the morning, and I'm writing this letter up on the bridge. I'm on watch, but I'm due to be relieved in fifteen minutes. These night watches are the best part of the day here in the tropics. The days are so hot they sap all one's energy, but the nights are cool and pleasant.

Tonight there's a big silver half moon overhead, and the whole bay is bright as day. On the starboard is the Big Dipper and on the port is the Southern Cross—a sight one never sees outside this tropical belt. Oh, there's no doubt about it—these tropical nights are beautiful. (Even so, that sack is going to feel mighty good.)

Your apartment sounds very attractive, Sparky, and I'm sure I'll like it no end. Only hope I get to see it in the very near future. So far, there's no dope on the transfer—but I still continue to anticipate one. What an optimist! Just keep your fingers crossed and one of these days I'll be breezing in to take you dancing—if you'll go. And, yes I do remember the sunburned kids and the New Year's dance. We did have fun, didn't we?

Good night, Carmen. Love, Harold. Capt. H. L. Hiner, U.S.M.C.

MARCH 19, 1944. CENSORED

Dearest Carmen,

Well, here I am back in New Guinea again after a ten-day recreation period in the Australian area. We had a wonderful time down there. The city is clean, beautiful, and utterly American; and the people are so friendly and hospitable. It is by far the most delightful port we have hit away from the States.

If we stay in this area very long, we all hope to get back down there again.

> Australia is indeed an oasis in an otherwise bleak area. The officers of the *Boise* are given honorary memberships in the Sydney Country Club while there and have no problem meeting girls.
>
> While the city is utterly American, some of the language is colloquial and the meaning of some words confusing. Harold has a date one evening and has to wait awhile for her to show up. She apologizes for being late and explains that the delay was caused because she had to stop on the way home and pick up her "screw." He is relieved to learn that is her pay-check.

Gad, but it was good to hear from you yesterday, Sparky. Received your letter of February 10th. Also received a letter from Butcher. According to his letter, he and Adrus are hilariously happy—he's such a wonderful fellow.

I've just heard from the folks, and they tell me that Jim was inducted around the middle of February. I had hoped he and Lillian would be left together, but I guess that was just too much. When the kids found Jim was to be inducted, they flew home so Lillian could meet the folks and see our beautiful country. They had about ten days, and I guess the folks just loved Lillian. I'm surely glad. It's so damned awkward otherwise. (If you notice any smudges, pay no attention. I'm writing, this with a blotter under my arm—clothed only in my birthday suit. The tropics would be uncomfortable in mixed company, for the only way to approach comfort is to expose all possible skin areas.)

As for the guard in your bank, we have a saying, "Once a marine, always a marine." No other service ventures as much. I, too, hope I meet him soon. Love, Harold

Dear Diary,

I'm glad to hear Harold finally had liberty in a location that resembles America. Most of his liberties recently have been in places where the women put red mud in their hair, are fat and naked to the waist, or chew betel nut, which blackens their teeth; or where the cities are filthy and the language foreign.

However, I must confess I have mixed feelings over his enthusiasm for Australia. The newsreels and newspapers have been reporting on our servicemen in Australia. Seems the women are beautiful and the parents anxious to have their daughters marry Americans. Harold mentioned they are hospitable. Word is that the men are frequently invited to stay in the homes and are extended "special privileges," whatever that means. The girls find the Americans are generous with their money and treat women more as equals than do the Australian men. A recent newsreel showed Australian war brides arriving in America, and I swear they were all pregnant.

I keep saying I want Harold to have fun, and I do. I'd be lying if I said I wanted him to have that much fun.

---

12 APRIL, 1944. CENSORED

Dearest Carmen,

I received your letter of 14 March—and I have great news to impart! My optimism finally paid off, for I have received my orders to Fleet Marine Force, San Diego. I have to wait aboard until my relief arrives, which should be around the end of April or shortly thereafter—and I'm homeward bound!

I couldn't be any more pleased with those orders if I had written them myself. I get a month's leave, AND I'm tickled pink. I'm going to get to visit Harriet and Jim and my new brother and sister this time. Haven't seen Harriet and Jim since I came into the Marine Corps. Jim was inducted about the middle of February, but I'm going to see him wherever he is. So, I will be seeing you in a couple of months or so. Guess you might as well send my mail home until further word, for I hope to be gone before a reply to this could reach me. Happy day!

Carmen, I'm so very sorry to hear that your cousin has been reported killed in action. I know how badly you all must feel, and there is so little one can say to soften such a blow. I sincerely hope this is the only notice your family will receive.

How did you enjoy "The Drunkard?" Surely hope you changed your mind and partook of the beer. It's so damned hot down here, I'd give a buck for a glass right now. Surely going to keep our refrigerator stocked when I'm on leave. My God, but it's going to be great to get home! In 30 days I'll be a full fledged civilian again—for a while.

I've heard from both the Butcher and "Fat Boy" Elkins. I expect to see Bob en route to the States. Boy, what a session that will be. Butch says Bob hasn't changed a bit—except that his high forehead is a little higher.

I've got to get hot now and write a pack of "V-Mail" to all the rest of my correspondents so they'll knock off sending my mail out here, or I'll still be getting old mail a year from now. So long for now. Love, Harold   Capt. H. L. Hiner, U.S.M.C.

The campaign against Western New Guinea begins in April and the *Boise* participates in all of the major operations of this campaign on covering, bombardment, and fire support missions. These operations include the sea bombardment of Aitape-Humboldt Bay and the Tanamerah occupation at Humboldt; the night bombardment of the Wakde-swar area; the Wakde-toem; and the Biak occupation.

General MacArthur summarizes the Biak campaign as follows: Our success here means the practical end of the New Guinea campaign. It has resulted in reconquest or neutralization of the Solomons, Bismarcks, Admiralties, and New Guinea. From the forward point reached by the Japanese, we have advanced our front approximately 700 miles to the north. These operations have effected penetration of the conquered empire Japan was trying to consolidate in the southwest Pacific. We have now secured bases of departure for the advance to Japans vital areas in the Philippines and Netherlands East Indies.

General MacArthur stands on the *Boise*'s deck, looking in the direction of the Philipines, remembering when he had promised, "I shall return."

Capt. Harold Hiner's replacement finally arrives, and he leaves the ship at Biak.

3 MAY 1944. V-MAIL. CENSORED

Carmen,

Just a short note to let you know I'm still sitting aboard here waiting for my relief to arrive (I presume you received my letter of a month ago informing you of my being ordered to San Diego). He should arrive soon now. I'm growing very impatient. I've been fully packed for a month now.

Think I told you Jim had been inducted. Haven't heard where he went. In fact, haven't received a solitary scrap of mail in seven weeks now. Should get some soon.

Be seein' you soon. Love, Harold

Dear Diary,

I can't believe we're finally going to see each other. It's been a year and a half since we were together in Salt Lake. I'm so excited!

I've been sad thinking about my cousin, Frank. He was flying his next-to-last mission over Italy when he was shot down. For a while he was listed "Missing"; now he's confirmed "Killed in Action." He was my favorite cousin. Teased me a lot, but took care of me. Even took me to dances when I didn't have a date in high school. He didn't have to go to war ... he was twenty-eight, married, and in an essential job, but he volunteered because he didn't want to be thought a draft dodger. I guess I shouldn't be impatient about Harold's delay. At least he's coming home.

15 JUNE 1944. EN ROUTE. CENSORED

Dearest Carmen,

On my way home at last!! I was detached on June 1st and, until three days ago, have been making my way by spurts and by layovers down the New Guinea coast. I'm aboard a transport and should arrive in San Francisco around the first of July. Guess I'll go home first to see the folks, then to Phoenix to see Harriet and her husband.

Also plan to see Jim if it is at all possible. Heard from

Father just before I left the ship, and he tells me Jim is in Amarillo, Texas, A.A.F. I presume he is a cadet.

I'll be by to see you on my way to report for duty in San Diego, so keep some time open for me. I have a lot of dancing to catch up on—if it meets with your approval.

As soon as I get my plans squared away in the States, I'll give you the dope. I'm going to be glad to be going back to the Marine Corps, though I've enjoyed my duty with the Navy a great deal and wouldn't trade my experiences for anything.

Guess this is a bit late for a birthday letter. I really expected to be back in the States for your birthday—and there wasn't anything I could do about it out here. At any rate—a belated Happy Birthday!

Of course, this letter won't be mailed until after we dock, so by the time you receive it, I shall have been in the States a day or so.

Well, Sparky, keep the home fires burning, and I'll be seein' you soon. Guess there must be something to that song "Wishing Will Make It So," 'cause I have been. Hasta la vista, Harold

———🎵———

A lovely big bottle of Joy perfume, purchased in the Panama Canal Zone, December 1943, for my Christmas present, arrived the week of my birthday. That's the way it is in wartime.

June 1945, General Douglas MacArthur aboard the USS Boise. *In deep thought as he looks toward Corregidor. His promise to return has been fulfilled.*

CHAPTER 8

Shattered Dreams

Dear Diary,

I'm on cloud nine thinking about Harold having duty in San Diego. All I can think about these days is seeing him, if only for a little while.

The last few months have been a roller coaster. For a while I considered quitting my job and going home to be with the folks. They haven't heard from Dick or Ham for quite a spell. The weather has been bad this past winter and spring. My dad is struggling to manage the farm and livestock work and has been riding the range alone in blizzards. Most days he rides into town at 3:00 P.M. in case there is mail from the boys, and then goes back out until the long day's work is done. Due to the size of his operation, he could have at least one of them deferred from service, but both wanted to serve, so he told them not to worry, he could handle it.

Dick is in England flying B-17s, making bombing runs over Germany. Ham is somewhere in the Pacific. Karl Burgess, who lived with us after his father died, is missing; shot down over France and we don't know if he's alive. Cousins Francis, Betenson, a B-17 co-pilot, and Leigh Lunt also are prisoners, shot down while flying missions over Germany. The folks live in fear of getting the same word about our Dick or Ham.

Now that Harold expects to have duty nearby at Camp Pendleton, I'm glad I didn't act too hastily and go home.

100

Especially since I just heard from the folks that Cleo Dix found three letters from Dick when he was sorting mail late last night. Where but Cedar City would anyone deliver mail at midnight

Second Lieutenant Richard (Dick) Leigh completes thirty missions, during which four of his crew were killed by antiaircraft and fighter fire. At the conclusion of these missions, he is flying his third B-17 ... the first two having barely made it back to home base, too badly shot up for further action. In less than a year, due in part to heavy losses of pilots, Lieutenant Leigh attains the rank of major.

On May 27, 1944, Major Leigh is awarded the Distinguished Flying Cross, with clusters. He weighs 130 pounds, down from 145 when he started his missions. Squadron Commander Major McRay asks him what he thinks he'd like to do now.

"Go home and see my wife and daughter, sir."

"Yeah, you do that and they'll give you two weeks' leave of duty and your ass will end up in a B-29 flying over Japan. There's a job open at 3rd Division Headquarters for an operations officer. You can do it, and I will recommend you."

Major Leigh becomes one of Gen. Curtis LeMay's three operations officers. His first duty is to fly LeMay from England to New York City for a secret meeting of the top brass. They fly nonstop in a B-17 equipped with extra fuel tanks in the bomb bay and wings, flying time eight hours each way.

Richard now has a two-room apartment ... bedroom and small sitting room with fireplace. He eats his meals in a kitchen that serves only fifteen officers, and his room is kept clean by a WAC. In addition to his duties in operations headquarters, he flies General LeMay and other high-ranking officers to the Riviera for R and R and to staff meetings in Europe.

It's a relief for the folks knowing Dick is no longer flying combat missions. Life is not without worries, however, for we aren't sure where Ham is ... somewhere in the Pacific flying L-5s.

JULY 18, 1944. AT HOME IN IDAHO

Dearest Carmen,

This is not to be a decent answer to your letters of April 22nd, May 27th, and July 5th. Rather, it is a short note to thank you for them and to impart a bit of rather bad news. This morning I received a change of orders. Instead of reporting to San Diego as my original orders called for, I'm now to report on August 8th to Command and Staff School at Quantico, Virginia. However, I'm *absolutely certain* that upon completion of the course (about five weeks), I will again be ordered to San Diego.

Sooooo—I'll be seeing you, but it will be a month and a half or so later than we had anticipated. Actually, as far as the course itself is concerned, I'm glad to get it, for it is a fine one and one for which there is generally some competition. I'm glad to have gotten it without requesting it. You'll note my address after August 8th on the envelope.

Well, Sparky, I've been busier than that whirling dervish since I got home. We've been to the Jackson Hole country and up into the Sawtooth country. Gad, but I do love these mountains!

I was surely glad to hear of Dick's decoration, promotion, and new assignment, and I know you all must be so proud of him. I hope you get such pleasant news from Ham soon, as well.

Keep hold of those rain checks for me, and I'll be calling for them in a few weeks. Love, Harold

15 AUGUST 1944
U.S.M.C. SCHOOLS, QUANTICO

Dearest Carmen,

I received your letter of the 11th yesterday. Thanks for the news. You're right about school, except I hardly think "entrenched" is quite the word! "Swamped" or "buried" would be closer. We have 52 hours of class per week—or over 8 hrs. a day, six days per week for every week of the twelve. So—there'll be little of the social whirl for us with only Sundays off.

It's really a fine course, though, and I'm glad to be here. Competition is pretty stiff, as we have more lieutenant colonels and majors than captains in the course.

Quantico itself is a beautiful old base, and our quarters are very comfortable. Two men per room, and my roommate is a former Basic School classmate. Good arrangement.

Heard from Elkins while I was home. Ran into John Hall, now an ensign, USNR, while in Arizona. He's stationed at Morro Bay and says he gets to L.A. occasionally. He asked about you and I gave him your address.

Well, Sparky, this school breaks up on Nov. 1, so hold onto that Cal weather and I'll be back out then. Love, Harold

15 SEPTEMBER 1944
STILL AT COMMAND AND STAFF SCHOOL

Dearest Carmen,

Thanks for your letter of 8/27. As you see, I'm a bit behind on my correspondence. School has not lightened its vigilance, and we are still digging. Guess this is one with no hump—all upgrade!

As for my staying in the Corps, Carmen, I have not definitely decided. It will depend entirely upon the situation at the end of the war. There is no other military organization which even approaches it in my estimation, and I really like the Corps and my work. At times, however, I find the many restrictions irksome. I'm too independent to like being told where I must be at what time the year around. It's necessary, of course, in wartime, but I don't think I'd enjoy it in peacetime. I sometimes wonder, though, whether I'm "independent" or merely "undisciplined." If it's the latter, perhaps I'll grow out of it eventually.

I'm very glad to hear of your new job, Carmen. It sounds as if your work would be a great deal more interesting. Hope you continue to like the owners, as well. Love, Harold

Dear Diary,

My new job is credit manager of Rhodes Jewelers on

Broadway. The owner, Mr. Schwartzmann, has been coming to my bank window to transact his business. One day, out of the blue, he offered me a job at a better salary than I'm getting at the bank, and I accepted. My friend Irys Hedman works for him also. The only hitch is his very possessive secretary, Teresa, is insanely jealous of Irys, and is horrified he'd hire another Gentile.

I like my work and it's interesting. We have a lot of servicemen and their girls coming in to buy engagement and wedding rings. Some of them act like they've just met. What gets me are the ones where the guy slips the ring on the girl's finger and says, "We's married."

2 OCTOBER 1944

Dearest Carmen,

Thanks for your letter of 9/21 and also Bob Hope's book. I really enjoy that character.

Yes, Sparky, I have seen Butch and Ad by now. They got four days' leave from the ship and came to Washington. We were swamped at school at that time, but I managed to do a bit of doubling up and got up to D.C. for their last night there. We talked a blue streak all evening. Butcher's still the same wonderful guy, only more so. The evening started off well at the Statler when the headwaiter and our waiter teamed up to spill our predecessors' remaining cream down the front of my greens—and I was so happy to see Butch I didn't even get mad. Surprised me no end.

Received news from Milt Merrill a week or so ago, as I suppose you did, too. Surely appreciated that letter, as it gave the most complete coverage on the grads I've yet come across.

Surely glad you're enjoying your work so much, Carmen. That's worth more than money—and nearly as essential, beyond a certain point, anyway.

Due to shortening of the course, it's been a bit heavier for the past couple weeks. From what we learn, instead of graduating on 1 Nov. as was originally planned, we are now to be available for shipment on the West Coast by 1 Nov. All scuttlebutt so far, though; and I'll let you know when I get definite word. Hope this doesn't sound too incoherent, for I've been writing like the devil to get this out during lunch hour. More later. As ever, Harold

Dear Diary,

Harold isn't being sent to San Diego, so we won't get to see each other as planned. A telephone call from San Francisco brings the disappointing news that he's been flown there, after only a few hours' notice, and will depart for Hawaii within the hour. I'm heartsick. The worst part is I know he'll be in combat before long. There must be a reason the course was cut short. I can tell when he knows he's about to go into combat. His letters get a little more formal and he ends with "As ever" rather than "Love." I can't decide if his feelings for me are changing or if he's trying to ease up because he thinks he might not come home all in one piece.

14 Nov. 1944. CENSORED

Dearest Carmen,

Look where I got stopped on my way "to war." By this time, I expected to be twice as far from the States, but when I reached Hawaii, they snagged me for the Marine Corps' highest staff this side of Washington. Didn't like it worth a damn at first, but I'm getting used to it now. Swell bunch to work with. Only thing is I'd requested a rifle company and sort of hated to be stopped clear back here in a job some married character should have. Guess my folks are tickled pink, though.

I don't expect to get back this time for at least two years and perhaps not until the end of the war. My biggest regret is I didn't get to see you last time back as I was sure I would. Marine Corps is in too big a job to trifle with me, though.

Well, Sparky, it's a sleepy night, so guess I'll turn in. As ever, Harold

In the fall of 1944, glider pilot Henry (Ham) Leigh becomes a part of the 310 Squadron of the 3rd Air Commando Group and is shipped out for Hollandria, New Guinea, to take part in the invasion of the Philippines. While at sea, the naval battle of the Philippines takes place, the Japanese navy is defeated, and there is no longer a need for gliders.

The glider pilots are transported by ship to the island of Leyte, arriving at the height of the rainy season. The two-man wall tents for the officers are useless on the beach, so are not unloaded until ten days later. Meanwhile, they sleep propped up against palm trees in the pouring rain.

Ground troops have advanced only 1,000 yards off the beach, so the Japanese are not far away. The men soon learn that the Japanese are not the only enemy. The first night on the beach, one of the glider pilots starts to scream. When his buddies crawl over to assist him, they find a ten-inch centipede latched on to his lower lip. Officer Leigh awakens the same night to a scraping sound on the box he keeps next to his bed. A flashlight reveals an enormous rat slowly dragging his .45 pistol across the box, determined to add it to the treasures in its nest.

When the rainy season abates, Flight Officer Leigh reports to Clark Air Base, about fifty miles north of Manila, where he is checked out in L-5s and other light planes. While there, he is ordered to fly to Luna Beach and report for duty to Colonel Volkman, commander of northern Luzon.

Colonel Volkman, an American officer, took to the hills when the Japanese took Luzon and became a leader of the guerrillas during the occupation. His army is virtually all Philippino, except for a few American officers and men needed for special services

Luna Beach is located between the small villages of Luna and Tagudin on the east coast of northern Luzon, halfway between Lingayan and Laoag. As a member of General Volkman's staff, Leigh shares quarters with another glider pilot, Flight Officer Hutchinson. A Philippino woman keeps the place clean and does their laundry, and they share the colonel's mess.

The problem facing the pilots is to figure out the best way

ocean, with dense jungle on one end and a 100-foot cliff on the other. A large river between the runway and the cliff empties into the ocean. The trees are so tall that it is impossible to fly over, get on the runway, and stop before you're in the river. The only feasible route is to come in low from the sea side of the cliff, do a small S maneuver when you get to the river, and land toward the trees.

Leigh admits he started out apprehensive (scared), but after a few landings it became routine. For takeoff he has his crew back the plane up to the end of the jungle. Then, with his brakes on full, he revs up the engine to full throttle and takes off toward the cliff. Without a passenger, he is airborne before he gets to the river, makes a small right to miss the cliff, and is out over the ocean. If he has a passenger, it's hairier. The high riverbank makes a good launching pad, and with a 185-horse-power engine in a small plane, he can ease it to the right enough to miss the cliff. His only worry is that the engine might sputter and he'll wind up in the river or the ocean.

Before long, Flight Officer Leigh is flying reconnaissance and courier service and transporting wounded from the front-line aid stations to the major hospital services. Aid stations knock out a dike on a rice paddy so the L-5 can land and take off. With room for one stretcher in the plane, the wounded are evacuated quickly.

Reconnaissance of enemy lines and supply routes requires the L-5 pilots to call for a flight of P-51s when they spot some-thing worth bombing, mark the target with smoke grenades, then make a mock run to show the P-51s the safest route to target.

17 Dec. 44

Dearest Carmen,
Hardly a day passes that I don't meet another old friend—Utah State friends, Salt Lake friends, Oklahoma City friends, and old *Boise* shipmates right and left. I don't know a place in the whole world where I'd see as many friends come and go as I do here. Surely is great to see them all.

Elkins is really in fine shape. It seems that after I saw him in Salt Lake—and before he reported to me here—he got engaged! He's hard-hit! Glad to hear you heard from Butch. He owes me a letter, and I'm going to give him hell if I don't hear from him soon.

Life goes on at the same even pace out here. Don't do much for excitement except meet some of the friends I run into for dinner, go to the beach occasionally, and sunbathe and work out quite regularly during lunch time. There you have my Hawaiian life for the most part. Throw in about 8 hours of paperwork daily, a dash of tennis, a few drinks here and there, an occasional dash around the island on business, of course, and you have the whole picture. Not exciting, but relatively satisfactory—for the time being.

Yesterday was a bright day. I ran into a fellow who was my closest friend in Salt Lake. We went to junior high, high school, and the first year of college together. Then I went to Logan and he moved to Wash., D.C. The next time I saw him was the summer of '39, when he was a ranger at our beloved Zion Canyon and I was Iron County Range Examiner (dropping the ball all over the place by not taking you out). I'd lost track of him then until yesterday—to find that he's a captain in the Marine Air Corps and the modest possessor of the DFC and the Air Medal. We surely had a celebration. He's a great guy!

Received a letter from my father yesterday, written in Omaha. He planned to stop in Denver on the way home to see Jim and Lillian. Surely wish I could have met my sister-in-law. Guess I'll meet her in another couple years or so—if those union characters back there wake up soon and begin to realize the tremendous job ahead of us in the Pacific. I honestly can't see victory here short of three years at best, and twice that if our war effort is tied down by a lot of union (blank blank).

Hate to fold on a sour note, Carmen, but think I'd better secure. Regards to your family. Merry Christmas, Sparky, and Best ever, Harold   Capt. H. L. Hiner, USMC

Dear Diary,

I can tell he's homesick and discouraged. I feel pretty much the same way. I guess it's the season. At Christmastime everyone wants to be home or with someone they love. I've decided I'm going to try to go home for the holidays. Mr. Schwartzmann will give me time off, and he believes he can get train reservations for me.

My last letter to Art Culver came back marked "Missing." It came in the same mail as a long, cheerful letter from him, reminding me of our horseback ride in Cedar. I keep remembering the last time I saw him and how sentimental he was about leaving. I wish I knew his folks and could find out more about his welfare. Truth is, I'm all mixed up. I feel guilty for some reason . . . I feel I let him down.

I am beginning to think this war will never end, that it will drag on, taking its terrible loss of life until my generation is old and gray. I wonder if I'll ever see Harold again. He obviously feels the war is far from over. I NEED to go home. I need to see my little hometown and our beautiful red hills set ablaze by the setting sun, eat my mother's cooking and hug my little brother

and sister to feel in touch with reality. Everything else seems transient and unreal.

Lt. Henry Hamblin (Ham) Leigh

Utah Fortress Pilot Cheats Nazi Gunners

April 20, 1944—AN EIGHTH AAF BOMBER STATION, ENGLAND—Fearless handling of the controls on the way to the target, a willingness to make a sacrifice at the target, and more nerveless handling of the controls coming back from the target brought the Eighth AAF Flying Fortress "Ice Cold Katy II" safely back to its base, badly shot up and with one dead crew member.

Flying the big bomber was 26-year-old Second Lieutenant Richard H. Leigh of Cedar City, Utah.

As the Fortress got near to its important target in southern Germany, 12 Messerschmitt 109s pressed home vicious attacks.

Fights Off ME-109s

"They came in one after the other, shooting cannon and machine guns at us," said Pilot Leigh.

But despite the savage swarm of swastika-painted fighters, the Utah pilot kept his ship in formation, maneuvered it cleverly as the big ship sparred with the diving and sweeping fighters. His gunners got two of the ME-109s. One of the nazis fell victim to the top turret gunner just before a direct hit on his position killed the gunner instantly.

Before the target was reached the fighters had punched holes into "Katy's" bomb bay, hit an engine and started an oil leak, mauled the stabilizer so that the controls were sluggish, and knocked out the oxygen to every position but Lieutenant Leigh's.

Gives Bombardier Oxygen

"I used the smallest amount of oxygen possible still left in the system, and when we got to the bomb run I cut my supply so the bombardier would have a full supply for the job of releasing the bombs," said Lieutenant Leigh. Other crewmen were using small emergency bottles.

After "bombs away," the bombardier removed the dead turret gunner from his position, and then had to rush back to the nose to help ward off more attacks as the crack German fighters tried to finish off the stricken ship.

"In the attacks coming away from the target," said the Utah pilot, "our astro dome was shot out, two big holes were opened in the wings, and one of the tires was shot up. I didn't know the tire was flat until I hit the runway, but the brakes were okay and that saved us from damage during the landing."

Second Lt. Richard H. Leigh, photo and article from the Salt Lake Tribune, *April 20, 1944.*

Harold at Command and Staff school.

Harold in group shot, Command and Staff school. He is at left, top row.

Above: *Kirk Stewart, Ray Miller, and Harold en route from Command and Staff school to FMF Pacific. Kirk was killed on Iwo Jima.*

Right: *Harold in Maui with the 4th Marine Division as OPNS officer.*

CHAPTER 9

Semper Fidelis
(ALWAYS FAITHFUL)

———🎵———

Dear Diary,

Mr. Schwartzmann did it! He got reservations for me on the train so I could go home for the holidays. I've worked for him only a few months, but he gave me a generous Christmas bonus as well. Going home for the holidays was wonderful. I'm the only girl in a club car full of young soldiers and business types.

Christmas Day we had our traditional tree, good things to eat, and a carol sing-along with Mom playing her beloved Steinway grand piano. Except for Dick and Ham not being here, it's perfect.

Returning to L.A. wasn't as easy as getting to Cedar had been. Dad would have to drive me to Lund, where the only train going to the West Coast would stop briefly at the ungodly hour of 11 o'clock at night. I would arrive in L.A. just in time for work, so I wore my new suit with hat and gloves to match and the shoes with four-inch spike heels. They're not very practical for travel, but I'll be sleeping most of the trip, so it won't matter.

There's no depot at Lund. When the train stopped, I jumped on and it took off the minute my feet hit the landing. I got the shock of my life when my eyes became accustomed to the dim lighting inside. The car was filled with disheveled, unshaven men in uniform. Tobacco smoke hung in a gray pall and the odor of liquor and unwashed bodies nearly knocked me over. I'm bombarded on all sides by cat-calls, whistles and re- marks—"Hi Red, where ya going ... need some help?"

This is a troop train, for God's sake! I'm supposed to be on a civilian Pullman car. The next car is a Pullman, also full of sol- diers. A bored porter escorted me to an upper berth already made up, threw my bag inside, helped me up the ladder, ac- cepted my tip, and with no explanation disappeared.

I was stunned. No way am I going to undress and get in bed. I sat there fully dressed and numb with shock. I tried to tell myself these men are occupied, and if I keep quiet they'll prob- ably forget I'm here. Boy, was I wrong!

Swisshhh! The curtain parted and a man, a cigarette dan- gling out of the corner of his mouth, grinned at me. I was pet- rified. He looked at me as if he enjoyed my discomfort, then held up a pack of cigarettes.

"No, thank you, I don't smoke." I started to smile, then thought better of it. Don't encourage him, but don't be rude. To my relief, the curtains closed.

I moved back against the outside wall to be as far as possi- ble from the opening. This couldn't be happening. Things like this didn't happen to young ladies from Cedar City, Utah.

Swisshhh again. A different guy, this one waving a flask at me, really smashed.

"Got some tequila here, wanta drink?"

"No, thank you, I don't drink." I sounded so prissy I wanted to laugh, except it wasn't funny.

"Well, now, how about some poker?" He stumbled back a bit, but righted himself. "You won't need no money, I'll back ya."

I didn't like the look on his face, or the way he looked at me. In spite of being fully dressed, I felt naked and vulnerable.

"I'm sorry, I don't play poker ... that is, I don't know how."

"Goddam, don't you do nothin'? The curtains snapped shut.

For the next hour, the interruptions were constant. Some, like the man who suggested poker, kept coming back. Now I was really scared. Some of these men looked out of control. Surely there were officers or noncoms in charge of this contingent, but where were they? I rang for the porter ... he didn't come

Then it hit me like a ton of bricks. I'm going to be raped ...

on a train, of all places. Oh, my God! I took off my shoe and stared at the heel. This is the closest thing I have to a weapon and by damn, I'll use it if I have to. I'll go for the face, or . . .

Again the curtains were jerked apart. I shrank back into the corner of the sleeper, wishing I could disappear into the night outside. The guy who had been the most obnoxious was standing on the lower berth, leering at me and trying to hoist himself up to my level. Before I could strike a blow, his fingers slipped off the edge of my berth and he vanished from sight.

"Goddam you son-of-a-bitch, let me go—butt out. None of your business, you bastard."

I didn't dare look out to see what was happening, but I knew from the cursing and scuffling in the corridor a fight was in progress, but I didn't know who was fighting whom or for what reason. I clutched the shoe in my still gloved hand, tears filling my eyes and choked back the sobs I knew wouldn't help. Finally, the noise stopped . . . I waited.

A face I hadn't seen before appeared outside my berth. This man was huge; he was older and towered above the others who had pestered me. He was a black man, and his face was scarred and mean-looking. The odor of liquor was so strong I felt sick to my stomach. I was rigid with fear and didn't realize the shoe with the dagger-like heel was still in my upraised hand.

"It's okay, ma'am; you ain't goin' to be bothered no more. I'll be sittin' down here watchin' out." His voice was deep and melodic, like a singer's voice. He closed the curtains quietly, and I heard the lower berth groan from his great weight.

The rest of the night seemed endless. I stayed wide awake wondering if I could trust this man I didn't even know? I've never known a black person. There are none at all in Cedar City. Why should he care about me?

Gradually the noise in the car ceased. The only sounds were snoring and the shuffling of cards by the man below . . . solitaire . . . I suppose.

When the train slowed down and the Los Angeles stop was called, I relaxed, freshened my makeup, and rang for the porter. The nightmare was over!

The big, black man, looking bleary-eyed with fatigue, was still there. He stood up and wearily stepped aside, his eyes downcast as I descended the ladder. The others were stirring in the car, getting ready to disembark.

"Thank you *very* much." I reached for his hand and squeezed it slightly. I very much wanted to express my gratitude in a more meaningful way, but had no idea what would be appropriate The big man was ill at ease, but I couldn't leave. I looked directly at him, still holding his hand, forcing him to look at me. I hoped my eyes would convey what I couldn't find the words to express.

"You're welcome, ma'am," he said. Still not at ease, he looked back at the floor.

I felt tired and a little shaken, but I have to be at work on time, so I ran for the streetcar and got aboard in the nick of time.

JANUARY 10, 1945

Dear Carmen,

Just received the fine billfold and lovely picture you sent me for Christmas. Thank you so much. I have a "feel" for good leather and that's the finest billfold I've ever had.

The picture was—or is—very attractive, and I'm so glad to have one of wallet-size. The other pictures I have of you are in the small album I carry—but this one stays in the wallet. Makes me even sorrier I was unable to see you last time.

Haven't received a letter from you for some time now. Believe I have written twice since last hearing from you. However, I'm used to irregular mails by now.

See Elkins quite frequently. He, Scherbel, Burl Hermansen, Karl Ward, and I spent all Sunday afternoon and evening together. Took a couple of nice drives, and I accompanied them to church (L.D.S.) in the evening. That place always looks like a gathering of USAC alumni. Our Butcher Boy has been transferred to some admiral's staff, presumably shore-based.

Life goes on in the same old groove here. With these regular hours, I feel like a businessman—practically! My work has turned out to be exceedingly interesting, and the officers with whom and for whom I work are a wonderful bunch, capable, efficient, and attractive. I really like my job now!

I'm afraid Jim is about due to ship out upon the expiration of his present furlough. Surely hate to see it. Don't mind staying out here much myself, but I hate to see my "little brother" taken from his wife.

Write soon and give me all the dope and thanks for thinking of me and for the picture and billfold. As ever, Harold

---

JANUARY 24, 1945

Dearest Carmen,

I was glad to hear of your visit to Utah. Have some interesting news that surprised me a great deal. It seems my parents are contemplating a move to Phoenix. The manager there is being transferred to Cleveland, and the company has offered father the state of Arizona, which has over twice the premium income of southern Idaho. Father has accepted, pending a personal check-up of the Arizona set-up.

More news, which you've probably noticed already, is that I made major—today.

I'm very sorry, Carmen, that you had to give up your apartment. I'm sure you must have made a delightful spot out of it. Wish I could have seen it last time. And there's no doubt you have just lost most of your privacy. Too bad, however it could be a lot worse. Give Sister Alice my love.

As concerns a snap, Sparky, I did have a few taken at Quantico and Annapolis recently. However, they're all with my gear elsewhere, and I can't enclose any with this letter. As soon as I can, however, and if there are any suitable, I'll send some. Incidentally, I don't think you'd particularly care for one of me as I stand today, as I had my hair cut off to ¾" a week or so ago and am again a "Heil Hitler" character. Gruesome is the word!

I didn't tell him about my train trip home from Utah. I didn't think he needed to know about that.

My roommate, Leora Petty, is getting married to Scott George, Butch Kimball's cousin. He just got back from three years overseas. I can't afford the apartment alone so will be moving into a larger one with three other girls. Alice Randall (Sister Alice), my Chi Omega friend from Ogden, Utah; Doris Lyngstad from North Dakota; and Ellen Swensen, a friend of Alice's, also from Ogden.

The new apartment is on 6th, across the street from MacArthur Park. We have a two-bedroom, living room, kitchen, bath, and balcony on the third floor. There is a lobby on the first floor manned by a security person and a streetcar stop out in front. It is nice, but not as charming as our little efficiency apartment on Westmoreland.

26 JANUARY

Here we go again. Some interruption that was!

Carmen, I can't tell you what I think of your work in the hospital. I know how trying it must be at times and what courage it takes—although I realize you're doing it simply because you're you!

Carmen, I have just learned this mail is not to leave the ship. So—I can now tell you we're underway for another blow, which will have been struck long before you receive this letter. This mail will be held until its release will not jeopardize our current operation. In the meantime, I'll no doubt be roundly cursed by all with whom I correspond as a "back-slider" and a poor correspondent. However, eventually this will be delivered, and my apparent negligence will be explained. Guess it will really be some time before we receive mail, though.

I've known for some time that I was to be allowed to accompany the staff on combat operations, and that knowledge has made staff work acceptable to me. I'm glad to be underway—though I guess the folks will hate it, having thought me securely tucked away here on Hawaii.

Take it easy, Sparky. Don't work too hard, and have fun! Regards to all the gals and family. Love, Harold, Major U.S.M.C.

Dear Diary,

I don't know why this is such a shock to me. I really didn't expect he would be kept in Hawaii indefinitely doing staff work, but I hoped he would.

At least he didn't end his last letter with "As ever." If he had, I think I would throw in the towel. I still get upset when he tells me to have fun. How can anyone have fun with the terrible consequences of war becoming more visible every day?

The hospital work I'm doing is in a rehabilitation center for the severely injured, in a suburb of Los Angeles. On Saturdays, I take a streetcar to a stop downtown where the volunteers are picked up and bused to the center. We do things for the patients like read to them, write letters, wheel them outside in a wheelchair if the weather is nice, or sometimes just visit with them. Some are blind, some amputees, and some badly disfigured.

By the time I leave there, I'm a wreck inside. I swear some of them don't look a day over sixteen.

The beginning of 1945 sees many changes in America's strategic position. In three years, the army has grown from 1,000,000 to 8,000,000 and the navy from 430,000 to 3,800,000. War production has increased by 680 percent.

The people of Japan have been led to believe their nation is impregnable, and that no foreign foot will ever step on the soil of their fortressed homeland. They are rudely awakened from their age-long fantasy when, during the last four months of 1944, American Superfortresses bomb some of their major industrial cities.

This became possible when the Allies took the Marianas, Saipan, Tinian, and Guam, from which our bombers can reach Tokyo. However, with Iwo Jima held by the Japanese, Tokyo is forewarned when our bombers are approaching. Planes crippled in battle aren't able to make it back to home base, and too many American million-dollar B-29s, with their crews of eleven men, are being lost.

An all-out assault on Japan itself can only be launched when American air bases are closer to Tokyo. Iwo Island, with its three airports all named Motoyama, only 600 miles from Tokyo, is obviously the essential springboard to final victory in the Pacific. The planning staff knows that a heavy price will have to be paid, for Japan has vowed to fight to the last man and no one doubts they will.

Maj. Harold Hiner is on the SS *El Dorado* on his way to Iwo Jima the latter part of January 1945. He is assigned to the Marine Corps Pacific Staff for the upcoming combat operation.

3 MARCH 1945

Dearest Carmen,

This is not to be much of a letter—just a quick flash to let you know where and how I am. I'm sure our delayed mail must have been released before now and you have no doubt deduced that I am in on the assault of Iwo Jima. We are on the downhill push now, and before long I shall be heading back to Oahu for a while. This has been the filthiest operation in the history of the Corps, and I'm glad to have been here, but we've paid a heavy price for a very unattractive piece of real estate. Of course, it has cost the Japanese even more.

We haven't received any mail for about six weeks until yesterday. Haven't heard from you or my parents yet, but I'm sure there are some letters from you all somewhere back along the line. I did hear from Harriet and Jim, and the folks have moved to Phoenix.

Well, Sparky, business is picking up a bit, so I'd better knock this off. Hope to hear from you very soon, but I'll drop you a decent letter in a couple days anyway as soon as the situation relaxes a bit. Love, Harold   Major H. L. Hiner USMC

Iwo Island has been bombarded for seventy-two days from the air and three days from the sea prior to the landing of the 4th and 5th Marine Divisions, with the 3rd Division to be landed two days later. Even so, Japan is too occupied watching the Philippines, China, Burma, and other areas, to suspect that the Iwo landings are so close.

One of the reasons Japan is oblivious to the imminent danger is the "Navajo code talkers," whose unwritten language the Japanese have not been able to fathom. The Marine Corps uses these Native Americans in communications, and the enemy has never been able to break their code.

Shortly before 9:00 A.M. on February 19, 1945, six battleships lead a parade of cruisers and destroyers headed for the Island of Iwo. It is a picture-perfect day; a tropical sun dances over the waves as the task force approaches. A young marine leaning on the rail of an assault transport is heard saying to his buddy, "What a perfect day to die."

Prior to landing, there is the usual checking of equipment and personnel, then the final piping of divine services: "Now, hear this. The smoking lamp is out. Knock off all card games. Knock off all unnecessary work about the ship and keep silence about the decks during divine services." Before the piping, other young marines have been baptized inside an LST's bow doors by Chaplain James Coffee.

The ships circle the island while hundreds of planes fly overhead. Both bombard the shore to make landing marines on the beach possible.

The island is small—only five miles long and less than two miles wide. The enemy there, estimated to be 15,000, is later discovered to be more than 20,000. They are hidden in an interlocking system of caves, tunnels, pillboxes, and blockhouses, almost one per man. There are 100 caves in one area 400 by 600 yards; some are forty feet deep. Two-story pillboxes are sunk into the volcanic sand. More than 115 guns are hidden in concreted positions on Mount Suribachi. The Japanese have added every known device to an already formidable fortress created by nature.

The Marine Corps finds itself in the toughest fight of its long career. The bombardment from air and sea has knocked out Iwo's air power and cut down much of the shore defenses, but it can't reach most of the skillfully hidden positions. Mines are strewn over the terrain, as are snipers and boobytraps. The marines, totally exposed, are forced to fight an unseen enemy that has every advantage.

It takes hours for the first waves of the 4th and 5th Marine Divisions to land. They face heavy fire and struggle in knee-deep volcanic sand to advance with their heavy equipment and supplies. One of the men looks around at the beach on which they are crowded and exclaims to his foxhole buddy, "God, what a place! What a dump! What a stinking hellhole!"

The beach is a depressing gray of volcanic ash. Once there were subtropical trees here, but the night chill has stunted them, and any foliage that might have existed has long ago given up. For wildlife, there is only one type of bird, a little like our rail. They add to the worries of the marines at night by standing like statues a foot away from occupied foxholes. One irate marine complains, "Those stupid-assed birds are giving away our position so they can eat us when the Japs shoot us." Nothing the men do has any effect on them.

Where sand is not the cover, volcanic rock has been piled from ancient eruptions. "Padre, after God got through making the world, he must've took all the dirty ash and rubble left over and made Iwo Jima" is the way one man put it, speaking to a navy chaplain.

Organized resistance ends at 6:00 P.M., March 16. The marines have lost 4,189 officers and men killed in the twenty-six-day action, 441 more are missing, and 15,308 are wounded. Of the six men who raised the flag over Mount Suribachi, only two are still alive.

Japan has believed Iwo impossible to take and warned that ten marines would die for every Japanese killed. Final accounting shows that six Japanese died for every marine death.

Not since Guadalcanal has the Marine Corps requirement that every marine must be a fighting marine first and a specialist second paid off as well as on Iwo. Pfc. Warren Gray is a cook who "had to be allowed into the lines," as his company commander put it, "when it looked for a while as if there would be nobody left to cook for." Gray's foxhole was on a knoll that faced the enemy positions. All night long, he directed mortar fire as the Japanese tried all their tricks in an attempt to infiltrate or counterattack.

Maj. Harold Hiner, who requested he be given command

of a rifle company rather than a staff job, is given duty on the beach in addition to his staff responsibilities. Countless others fill in where needed—cooks, corpsmen, forward observers, even medics and division correspondents ... four clerks from one division-supply section volunteer for front-line duty. Within forty-eight hours, one is missing and the other three are wounded. These men, and the others who lived, could never forget the dead marines, stacked up like cordwood on the beaches, nor the night cries of the Japanese: "Marine—tonight you die!"

Never in their 168-year history has the Marine Corps' motto "*Semper Fidelis*" (Always Faithful) been put to the test so completely as in the fight for Iwo Jima.

When Major General Erskine dedicates the Third Division's cemetery on Iwo, he says: "Of the cost to us in quality! No one will ever understand who did not fight side by side with those who fell.

"Let us do away with names, with ranks and rates and unit designations, here. Do away with terms, regular, reserve, veteran, boot, old timer, replacement. They are empty, categorizing words which belong only in the adjutant's dull vocabulary. Here lie only, (pause), only Marines."

I'm haunted by a drawing that has been appearing in quite a few publications lately. It depicts a young, battle-weary marine. The caption reads: "When he goes to heaven, to St. Peter he will say—another marine reporting—I've served my time in hell."

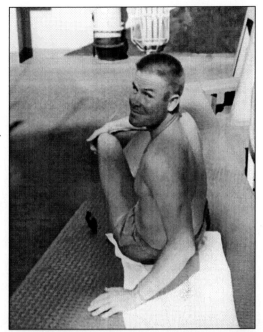

Right: *Harold on the deck of the USS* El Dorado, *on the way to Iwo Jima.*

Below: *Carmen (right) with new roommates Alice Randall and Doris Lyngstad, in McArthur Park across the street from their apartment house.*

This remarkable picture of the marines raising Old Glory on the summit of Mount Suribachi, Iwo Jima, is an enlargement from a sixteen-millimeter movie frame exposed by Marine Combat Photographer Sergeant William H. Genaust on February 23, 1945. Sergeant Genaust was attached to the Fifth Marine Division and worked shoulder to shoulder with Associated Press cameraman Joe Rosenthal at the time of the historic incident.

CHAPTER 10

Back from Hell

Dearest Carmen,

Our backlog of mail for the latter half of January and February finally broke through the day before yesterday, and I found I had a Valentine from you and your letter of 17 February. It was great to hear from you, Sparky, and I really appreciated the valentine.

Yes, Carmen, I was wondering how you heard so soon of my promotion. You should have heard from me soon after, though I'm not sure just when they did release our mail. We are now on our way back to Oahu. Gad, Carmen, this paragraph is disjointed, but there are a couple of seamen literally pounding a desk to pieces right behind me, and I can hardly think.

In this last flurry of mail, I received my first news of home since the middle of January and quite a lot has occurred. The folks moved to Phoenix. Harriet says the home they bought is the most "homey" house they've ever owned.

Your Sundays and the weather there sound delightful. Wish I could be there. At least the weather at Iwo Jima was welcome, being appreciably cooler than we had on the way out. Something else that sounds good is that talk of the marvelous cooks abounding in your apartment. You may be sure I won't pass up an opportunity of checking that out the very first chance I get. Love, Harold

127

Thank God, he's left that horrible island. From the reports on the radio and in the newsreels—and the press—Iwo must be a piece of hell on earth. I'm grateful he got through that ordeal unharmed, and feel so sad for those who didn't.

---

26 MARCH 1945

Hi, Sparky, darlin'

Back on Oahu and busy as hell. Getting transferred to the 4th Marine Division over on Maui and have a lot to do before I shove off.

Found your wonderful letters of 26 Feb., 5th, 9th, and 15th March letters here, and your letter of 17th March arrived today. Also received your Easter card. Thanks so much for all the mail, Carmen, for as I've told you before, it's the only thing that counts much with us out here.

Just returned from the club and am probably a bit canned, but I wanted to talk to you, so if this is too bad toss it overboard and another will be forthcoming just as soon as I can write.

In one of your letters you mentioned sitting up listening to the music that comes on late at night—"That Old Black Magic." Reminded me of the many nights back at school when I'd whip down to Heb's for half a dozen cups of coffee about 10 o'clock, then sit up and study all night while the house was quiet. I'd turn the radio on low to some California station, then when I'd begin to get stale, I'd get up and dance around the room for a while— thereby waking myself up and, at the same time, teaching my- self to dance. Remember the night we went down to the high school prom—and no one bothered us all evening. That was a good night!

By now you've probably gathered I'm presumptuously try- ing to answer all your wonderful letters with one foul one— since, being in the midst of a transfer, I don't know just when I'll be able to write again.

Hope you're still with me. The last few paragraphs sounded logical as I wrote them, but now I wonder. Looks a bit as if I might be swacked. Hear some radio somewhere playing "Lovely Hula Hands. " Lovely!

Sounds as if you all had a rugged session around there. Know how Alice felt with her cracked toe. Think I wrote you about a year ago that after two years in war zones, I ended up flat in my pack with—a cracked toe. What an ass!

Yes, Sparky, I saw *Keys to the Kingdom* before we went to Iwo and enjoyed it a great deal. I thought it very well done—I'm a horrible softie, in the dark of a theatre. Small heroics appeal to me so much more than the big flashy ones. (Sparky, if you're still with me, you're a wonder! I'm writing this as if I were talking to myself.)

Well, Carmen, this has become quite a bulky and involved epistle, so I'll secure. Love, Harold

Maybe I'm jumping to conclusions, but I detect a wistfulness in this letter. I can well imagine how much he'd like to come home before, as he puts it, "shoving off" again. I wonder where the next destination will be?

Sometimes I wonder why I fell in love with someone so unattainable—yes, I admit it, I AM IN LOVE. Could be he's found someone who is more accessible—there are lots of service women in the islands now. Maybe he regards me as just a good friend. I know I'd feel better if he complained occasionally.

Truth is, in these outlandish times, it's not difficult to find someone if you are open to the people around you. Everyone seems to be desperately looking for someone to care about. Maybe we should live for today and let tomorrow take care of itself. There must be something wrong with me. I'm in a rut.

3 APRIL 1945

Dearest Carmen,

I received both your letter of 27 March and your birthday package yesterday. Thanks so much for both of them. The birthday gifts were particularly well chosen, since cribbage is my favorite game and I really enjoy H. Allen Smith. So—thanks again, Sparky. It was really sweet of you.

Gad, that dinner you were preparing for Easter Sunday sounded terrific! That's quite a team of cooks you have there, including the boys from below. Sounds like fun. Did you get those pictures? If so—may I have some???

At present, I'm still standing by here waiting for transportation to the 4th Marine Division. Should leave within a day or so. As ever, Harold.

13 APRIL 1945. 4TH MARINE DIV. CENSORED

Dearest Carmen,

I have a very hazy notion as to what was included in my letter of March 26th, but from the tone of yours, I presume it was acceptable, thank God. May I ever be so lucky! You're a good woman, not at all surprised to find that out (again).

All I'm officially allowed to say of my new location is that I'm "somewhere in the Central Pacific Area." I've become a field soldier at long last and am living in a tent, showering and shaving in cold water, etc. Guess it's good for me. I'm afraid I was getting soft and lazy with all that barracks life.

Boy, I really let this short hair of mine down in the last letter, didn't I—telling you of my all-night "dance and study" sessions at the Sigma Nu House and that I was a "movie softie" all in one letter! I'm a ruined man.

Enough for now, Sparky darlin'. Will write again soon—when I get my new job. Love Harold, Major USMC

23 APRIL, 2ND BN, 25TH MARINES,
4TH MAR. DIV. CENSORED

Dearest Sparky,

This is not a letter—only a note to let you know I've been assigned and I'm so busy getting broken into my new job right now I can't call my soul (if any) my own.

My job is that of operations officer and third in command of a battalion—something over 800 men. It's one of the best jobs possible and I'm very happy to land it, but right now it has me damned near snowed. So many new phases and aspects I've never encountered!

However—just as soon as the pressure lets up a bit, in the next few days, I'll drop you a decent letter. Think I have a slight mail foul-up anyway, since I haven't heard from you since I last wrote—a week or ten days ago. Expect to get that squared away in a day or so. Love, Harold USMC

April 26, 1945: After twenty months of fighting, the historic Italian cities of Verona and Genoa fall to the Allies.

Benito Mussolini begs the Germans to save him and is given a place in a convoy headed for Germany. Before they can get out of Italy, partisans intercept the convoy and detain the hated dictator and his mistress, Clara Petacci. He is tried at once and, when informed of the verdict, whispers to one of his captors: "Help me and I will give you an empire."

Trembling and whining, Mussolini is tied to a chair, facing its back. He and his mistress are executed along with Achille Starace, once the leader of the Blackshirt Militia, and other Fascists captured by the partisans.

When the first Allied units reach Milan, they discover Mussolini and his mistress hanging, head down, in the Piazza Loreta and an angry mob shouting their hatred and abusing the lifeless bodies.

On May 1, Von Vichinghoff Scheets' emissaries meet secretly with the Allied chiefs and sign an act of unconditional surrender, effective two days later.

Dear Diary,

When the news of the surrender of Italy hit the papers, I couldn't help but think of my cousin Frank, who was shot down over Foggia, Italy. I adored him and thought he was the most handsome man in the whole world, until I met Harold. He knew I yearned to be more voluptuous and beautiful and I knew he loved me as a sister. However, he couldn't resist teasing me about my freckles and long, skinny legs.

I can close my eyes now and see him as he was the last time we were together, four years ago. I was in college at Logan and he was married, living in northern Utah. As soon as war was declared, he volunteered for the air force. He came home on his last leave before going to Italy the same day I got home for summer vacation. The next morning I was sleeping in, when awakened by his booming voice at the foot of the stairs to my bedroom.

"Carmen, get on down here—or I'll come up there and yank your lazy body out of that bed!"

I fairly flew out of bed, put on my most fetching morning outfit, did a quick makeup job, took two deep breaths to compose myself and appear unhurried. I descended the stairs as I had practiced at the Chi O house—the descent calculated to show my more mature figure and a smile on a face almost absent of freckles—thanks to a little makeup.

I will never forget the look on his face as I made my grand entrance. He stared at me, not saying a word, until I reached his level

"My God, you turned out to look like SOMETHING after all. I heard you were home. I wanted to see you and the sun on these good old red hills once again, so here I am."

I can't believe he's gone. Shot down in flames and I'll never see him again. The War Department is not sure, but they believe a body recovered in the area where he went down is his. They contacted his mother and offered to send the body home. Aunt Alt accepted, since there is a good chance it is Frank. She'll bury him alongside his father and brother. If it isn't he, then some other mother's son will have a well-tended resting place in peaceful surroundings.

8 MAY 1945. CENSORED

Hi, Sparky darlin',

It's more than presumptuous of me, but I'm going to try to

answer all your wonderful letters with this one. Believe me, Carmen, had I more time, I'd never do it, but—I'm really busy these days. And, besides, this "tent life" is not at all conducive to writing. I know the notes I've dropped you since my arrival here have been far from satisfactory and a very poor return for the sweet letters I received. I'll try to be more prompt and a little less close-mouthed in the future than I've been for the past month. However, as I indicated, correspondence is a bit difficult under field conditions.

This camp is rather primitive. It is either horribly dusty or terribly muddy. I believe I prefer the mud. At least you don't have to breathe it or wipe it out of your ears! And another thing—a two-faucet system is unheard of around here. The single gives only cold—very cold—water. I don't mind it for showering, as I always take a cold shower anyway; but I do definitely hate the stuff for shaving.

Of course, I'm still living in a tent (as we all do and will continue to do until we trade them for something less satisfactory). Actually, Sparky, I think the "back to nature" movement is good for me. I'm afraid shipboard and barracks life would have completely softened me before much longer.

As for the island itself, it is very beautiful—the most beautiful I've seen in this area. Our camp is situated up on a slope above the sea and the view is simply terrific.

Guess this is a happy day for you all. V-E day! I'm surely glad for your sake. Now Dick can come home. It didn't cause even a flurry of excitement in this camp, however, for we all know we have a long haul ahead. Of course, it means so much to us that all effort will be directed into this theater now, but it was greeted with a sober, quiet satisfaction rather than hilarity.

You mentioned the death of President Roosevelt in a recent letter. I, too, was deeply grieved at his death. I've always considered him a great man. I disagreed with his labor and domestic policies, but believed in his foreign policy—and believed in his sincerity in all things. He was a great and strong man, and his leadership will be greatly missed in the period we are entering.

About this "short hair business"—I'm sure that's the way it will be when you see me next, for I swear it will take an "I do" to make me let it grow again. I hate to wash it when it's long, because you know that old song, "I can't do, etc."

Well, Carmen, it's almost 0100 and I'm off for the field for the rest of the week, bright and early in the morning, so I guess it's time for me to fold. Hope this has made partial amends for my recent neglect. Goodnight, darlin', Harold

---

The 4th Marine Division, like countless other military units of the army, navy, air force, and marines, are gearing up for the final, most critical stage of the War in the Pacific. Operation Olympics, as the invasion of Japan will be known, and the total defeat of its treacherous regime will be the most brutal battle ever fought in the history of mankind.

The capture of Iwo Jima and Okinawa made it possible for the Superfortresses to increase in number and power, so that the original flight of eleven planes carrying scarcely 100 tons of bombs grows to a force of 820 Superfortresses that unleashes 6,600 tons of demolition and firebombs on a series of targets over Japan.

When Admiral Halsey takes over the third fleet again on May 28, 1945, Japan is already under attack from the sea. In the midst of raging typhoons, 105 American warships and 28 British combat vessels draw the net tighter. This armada shoots down 290 planes in combat, destroys 1,301 on the ground, and damages 1,374 more. Forty-eight enemy warships are sunk and 1,500 merchantmen sunk or damaged.

The time is drawing near for the actual land invasion to take place. Major Hiner and the countless other men who know what they will be called upon to do have few illusions as to their future. Japan vows to fight to the last man. The Allies have every reason to believe them.

Darn, I missed the volunteers' bus leaving the rehab center so will have to wait in the lobby for the next one. I'd better not miss that one, or I'll be here all night.

I'd give a lot for a cup of coffee, but all that's left in the volunteers' lounge is about a fourth of a cup—and it's so strong and stale I might have to eat it with a spoon. Oh well, better than nothing.

"That doesn't look too appetizing. If you'll step into the doctors' lounge, there's a fresh pot, and you're more than welcome to have all you want."

I recognized Dr. Bradford, who is one of our floor doctors and an administrator. "Thanks, it's been a long day." I followed him across the hall to the lounge, helped myself, and was surprised when he walked back to the lobby with me.

"You're Miss Lee, I believe?"

I explained that my name is pronounced like "sleigh," though most people who see it written give it the English pronunciation, which is Lee. He is through for the day and chooses to sit down and talk to me until the last volunteer bus arrives. He's tall and *very* attractive, seems like a nice man, I imagine in his 30s—probably married. He praises the volunteers profusely, so I leave feeling appreciated and complimented.

When I got home from work the following Friday, the phone was ringing.

"Paul Bradford here."

He wants to take me to dinner tomorrow night, after my shift at the center. I'm so surprised I find myself stumbling over lame excuses that don't make sense . . . even to me. I feel foolish, because it's obvious I'm rattled and not being entirely truthful.

"Miss Leigh—it is Carmen isn't it? Really, I'm not a bad sort—won't you give me a chance?"

"Well," I take a deep breath, "to be honest, I wonder if you are married. I don't go out with married men." I'd already been caught fibbing, so I decide telling the truth might make up for it.

He laughed, "No, I'm not married. If you prefer, think about it and give me an answer tomorrow. We can go someplace near the center for dinner, then I can drive you home, unless you decide you don't trust me and would rather I put you on a bus . . . it's your choice. I looked you up in the files and you don't live far so, either way, it's up to you. Please say yes."

I wore a suit and high heels and carried my uniform to the

center the next day. Just to be sure, I asked the floor nurse if Dr. Bradford is married, and if she knows how old he is.

"No, he's not married, and I'm surprised, as good-looking as he is. All the single nurses would give their eye teeth for a date with him. I'd guess he's in his early to mid-30s."

I accepted his invitation, then worried about it all day as I went about my work. I can't believe I said yes. What will we talk about? He's a doctor! We have nothing in common.

Every time I see him in the halls, I'm tempted to say I've changed my mind, but I'm intrigued and yes, bored. Besides, from everything I've seen about him, I think he's a gentleman and not like "Old Doc," who has only one thing on his mind. After all, it's just a date. When he finds out what a prude I am, he'll probably never ask me out again. I'm sure he knows plenty of sophisticated women nearer his age.

I changed into my suit and heels and met him in the lobby. When he saw I was not in my uniform, he looked pleased.

"This calls for a change of plans ... I need to think of a restaurant worthy of you, and I know just the place."

He was driving his own car, and the place was close by. It's at the top of a large building, guarded by a doorman who let us in without question. It looks like I've imagined a private club in the city would look, which no doubt caters only to members. There were others there, of course, obviously professional people. Several spoke to him, calling him Paul, and stared at me, the interloper. We are seated at a window table, overlooking the city.

I'm glad I came. I really have been lonely and kind of blue lately. I guess this is what Harold means when he says "have fun."

After we ordered a drink (I promised myself I would have only one), he turned quizzical, "Now, turnabout is fair play. Are YOU married?

It never occurred to me he might think that. But why not? Lots of girls are married with husbands overseas. In my experience it doesn't prevent a lot of them from dating, though it certainly would me. "No, I'm not."

"Have you ever been? And before you answer, I will tell you I have, while in medical school. It didn't last long, but made me a bit gun-shy, I guess."

"No, I haven't, but I am serious about a marine I met in college. He just got back from Iwo Jima, and is now attached to the 4th division, which I'm certain is preparing for the invasion of Japan. I haven't seen him since January of 1943.

The preliminaries over, I found him easy to talk to. We had a wonderful dinner and lots of laughs ... I like his sense of humor. He put himself through medical school playing with some of the big bands of the '30s. He plays the trumpet and also sings. He was amused when I told him about my mother who played piano in a dance orchestra at the age of nine and for the silent movies after her marriage.

He knows I share an apartment with three other girls, so I thanked him in the lobby and said good-bye as I pushed the button for the elevator.

"Carmen, you haven't seen the last of me, if I have anything to say about it. I've had a delightful time, thanks."

I really don't think he'll ask me out again, and I hope he doesn't. As much as I would enjoy his company, it can't go anywhere, and I'm sure he has better things to do with his time. On the other hand, it really is a pleasure to go out occasionally with a man, and I do believe he's a gentleman.

CHAPTER 11

On the Brink

Dear Diary,

On the streetcar coming home from work, I thought about my plans for the weekend. I'm taking this Saturday off from duty at the rehab center, and Old Doc is taking me and my three roommates to the beach. Whoopee!! The last few months have been difficult with Harold being at Iwo and not knowing what's going on with Ham. I treated myself to a new swimsuit for the occasion, and I'm going to relax and think of absolutely nothing—except making sure none of us is left alone with Doc.

Usually being the first one home after work, it's my job to pick up the mail at the front desk. Tonight there's a rather large package addressed to me. I expected to see my mother's handwriting, but instead the address is printed and the fancy return sticker is from a shop in Beverly Hills.

Inside are three layers of the fanciest-looking candy I've ever seen. The box is beautifully decorated and has a lock and key ... obviously intended to be used as a container for keepsakes, or who knows what. It is lovely! Inside the box is an envelope.

Dear Carmen,
Thank you for a great evening. I'm out of the city for two weeks. Will be back next Wednesday. I'm hoping you will consent to accompany me to an uncle's birthday celebration, Sunday evening the 20th.

I will call as soon as I get home. *Please* save that evening for me. I will explain further when I talk to you. Sincerely, Paul Bradford.

---

23 MAY 1945. CENSORED

Hi, Sparky,

And thanks so much for the snaps and the letter. They look mighty good to me. Only wish I might have taken the pictures.

Incidentally, Carmen, you may set your mind at rest on one point—I definitely shall not launch a "one-man" invasion of Japan." I admit I've pulled some crazy tricks in my time and that I do sometimes seek solitude, but—I'm not that far gone. However, to be sure, I shall write just as often as possible.

Yes, Carmen, this island is beautiful, and particularly so tonight. I just made a quick run down to my tent—and was spellbound by the beauty of the night. There is almost a full moon, not a cloud in the sky, and the sea below and the mountainside above are bathed in moonlight. Gad, but it is lovely; if they'd only run about thirty thousand service personnel, with all their hustle, and hurly-burly, right off the island and let the whole place relax, it would again be truly delightful, as I'm sure it was in peacetime.

I sincerely hope that by the time you receive this Dick is home. You all must be simply overjoyed. Now to get Ham and Jim home. I presume Ham is still flying L-5s in the Philippine Islands. Is that correct?

Well, Carmen darlin', it's high time I folded this and headed for my tent. Love, Harold   USMC

In June of 1945, most military units in the Pacific are being readied to participate in the upcoming assault on Japan.

Colonel Volkman and his guerrillas in northern Luzon are holding the area with the aid of American pilots who fly reconnaissance, mark targets, bring in supplies, and evacuate the wounded.

The time has come to make an assault on the Japanese-held ridges, and Volkman wants to get a look at their defenses. Flight Officer Leigh makes the first pass at 1,000 yards parallel to the ridges, as he had done on previous inspections. Volkman points to a specific area, saying he wants to fly closer to get a better look. Leigh gains altitude, heads straight for the ridge, then makes a diving turn to pick up speed. Still flying parallel, his right wing only fifty feet from the ridge, they are so close that the eyeballs of the Japanese defenders can be seen. Some are running along the trenches and others swinging their rifles to get a shot at the intruders.

Volkman doesn't say a word, just stares out the window until the end of the pass. When Leigh puts the plane into a tight, diving turn to move away from the ridge, Volkman explodes, "Jesus Christ! I didn't mean I wanted to shake hands with the Japs!"

After minutes of silence, Leigh asks if he'd like to make another pass. "Hell NO, I've seen plenty." When they land, Volkman walks away without a word. The next day, however, he again requests Officer Leigh to fly him to Manila, so he can confirm his plans with General MacArthur's staff.

Volkman is known to be a man of few words. During the return flight, though, he expresses his appreciation for the work the L-5 pilots are doing and asks Leigh how long he's been a flight officer.

"Two and a half years, sir. A lot of higher-ranking officers joined the glider program when it started, so now it has been dropped, there isn't room for any more in the Table of Organization. I expect to end my service as a flight officer."

They are in Manila two hours, then fly back to Luna Beach. Volkman, in deep thought until just before they land, remarks, "Incidentally, Leigh, you will soon be a second lieutenant."

"Thank you, sir," says Leigh, but he has his doubts that MacArthur's staff will actually follow through with it. Promotion requests usually come from a man's own squadron and take a long time to process.

August 1, orders making Flight Officer Ham Leigh a second lieutenant came through, having become effective three weeks before. Shortly thereafter, his squadron leaves for the island of Ie Shima, where they will practice landing their small planes on an aircraft carrier in preparation for the invasion of Japan. Plans are to anchor a carrier in Tokyo Bay from which their small planes can take off and land.

---

8 JUNE 1945. CENSORED

Dearest Carmen

Am more than a bit behind on the correspondence again—but I've read and appreciated all your letters so much.

Perhaps by the time this reaches you, Dick will be home. I surely hope so. That's as terrific a birthday present as you could possibly have. Which leads me to "Happy Birthday, Sparky." This will be a bit late, but I surely hope you do have a happy birthday and many happy returns.

Your life there certainly sounds attractive, Carmen. Beach, suntan, dutch-lunches, portable barbecues, bridge, and all the rest! Surely will be glad when I can participate again; drive up Logan Canyon, hike up East Rim Trail in Zion Canyon—and all that goes with these. Ho hum! There I go again.

Well, Carmen, guess it's high time for me to fold this and turn in. 'Night for now. Love, Harold

---

27 JUNE 1945 CENSORED

Dearest Carmen

No, I haven't been lost in the wilderness—quite. But for the last twelve days we've been out in the field on bivouac, with absolutely no opportunity to write. And in the morning, we return to the field again for another five days. So, with your letters of 8, 14, and 18 June before me, I figured I'd better dash off a line tonight. Understanding though you are, I know there's a limit to everything.

As for the flowers, Sparky, you're a thousand times welcome. I *did* wonder who the "thorn" was. Thanks for the dope. Wish there had been another thorn there and I had been "it." And—I wish I could see the tan you're cultivating. My own is terribly "undernourished" right now except for face and hands.

Was glad to note in your letter of the 18th that you have not become anemic. I have absolutely no use for artificial, neurotic women. I'll take a good, healthy mountain gal.

Well, darlin', guess I'd better secure this for tonight. Will write again as soon as we return from the field.

Love, Harold   USMC

The flowers were for my birthday, June 9 ... a dozen red roses. The "thorn," of course, is Old Doc, who took us to the beach, and the pictures he mentioned are the ones Doris took.

I admit when Doris took a picture of me in my new sexy black swimsuit, I tried my best to look fetching. From what he said about not being anemic, I think he noticed.

11 JULY 1945. CENSORED

Dearest Carmen

This leaves me on the last morning of a five-day leave in Honolulu. Take a plane back about noon. Talk about complete rest and relaxation. This has been just that. I came over alone and have been able to do just exactly as I wanted all the time.

I spent two days with one of my old shipmates, whose wife is a Honolulu girl. They live with her parents, and they have a beautiful little blond boy about 18 months old. Surely was pleasant to spend some time in a lovely home again. Makes my tent even less attractive.

So, you're apartment hunting again? Those wedding bells surely keep breaking up your apartments, don't they? Hope you and Doris find what you really want. With the time you have, you should have a pretty good chance.

And yes, Sparky, I do like wine with dinner, so that's a real date.

Well, Carmen, guess it's about time to fold my bag and take off for the airport. Hope I have a letter from you waiting for me over there. Love, Harold

———— 🖐 ————

Dear Diary,

Don't know where "over there" is. Some island out in the Pacific. Probably one of those recently taken from Japan. He's beginning to sound tired and homesick. He doesn't complain. Almost wish he would. He certainly deserves some leave, but why can't it be in the States? I'm worried—sounds as if he's about ready to go back into combat, and this time it will be as a foot soldier. I can't stand to think about it, yet I can't think of anything else. I need to get out and do something beside worry.

All day today, Thursday, I've been mentally rehearsing what to say to Dr. Bradford when he calls. He asked me to call him Paul, but it doesn't come easy—especially at the center. I enjoyed the evening we spent together, but going to a party at the home of people I don't know is something else.

Actually, I can't imagine why he's interested in me. I've made it clear I'm serious about someone else. With the scarcity of eligible men, he's bound to have women standing in line to go out with him.

The phone rings; it's him.

"Carmen—how are you? It's great to hear your voice. Paul Bradford here. I trust you received my note and hope you saved next Sunday for me.

"I'm fine—and thanks for the lovely box and delicious candy. I trust you removed the calories."

"Oh, you women—just like my aunt. Sunday is my uncle's birthday and she is having a cocktail party for him. They think of me as a son and insist I come by and hope I'll bring a friend ... they worry I'm turning into an old bachelor. Aunt Eleanor is always scolding me about the women I date. I want her to meet you because I know she'll be impressed. We wouldn't have to stay long, just drop in for a while then go on to dinner."

"Paul, I honestly feel I would be intruding on an occasion that should include only family and friends. Besides, I'm not often invited to cocktail parties, and I'm not sure I have anything suitable to wear."

He listened to the objections I could think of, then quietly voiced his rebuttal.

"Carmen, I feel we got off to a good start by being honest with each other. I know you are serious about a young man overseas. I respect that. Believe me when I say I enjoy your company and want to know you better. There are no strings attached to our friendship, but I'd consider it a favor if you would say yes for Sunday. I know my aunt Eleanor will like you and might quit scolding me."

What to wear! Being a girl means I'll spend a lifetime wondering what to wear. A suit is always a good choice—better to be underdressed than overdressed. That's what I plan to wear until the last minute. Then, on a whim, I put on the black dress with the lace insert at the neckline I wore the last time I saw Harold in Salt Lake. I haven't worn it since. Paul said I looked smashing.

I've never been to Beverly Hills, only heard how ritzy it is. The drive over was beautiful, and when we entered the driveway, I was in awe of the house. I could hardly wait to see inside. It sits on a hill and is mostly glass along the front, and inside you have the feeling of being outside. The furniture is large and comfortable, upholstered in muted colors.

Paul's aunt and uncle are attractive and seemed glad to meet me. Their friends are younger than I expected and, though I'm obviously the youngest person in the room, I soon feel comfortable participating in the conversation, which is stimulating and a change from the discussions I have with my contemporaries.

Paul's aunt and uncle lost their only son during the bombing of Pearl Harbor. She asked if I have siblings in the service. When I told her my two brothers and thirteen first cousins were all in the air force, and every young man I knew in college also in some branch of the service, her eyes teared. She complimented me on my work at the center.

On the way to dinner, Paul pointed out his apartment, which is in a nice area, close to his favorite restaurant. Again, all the patrons appeared to know him and gave me the once-over.

The menu was unusual, with entrees new to me. Paul, seeing my confusion, offered to order for me. Good idea!

"Carmen, I had my eyes on you for several weeks before approaching you at the center. I couldn't help but notice how the patients warmed up to you, especially the younger ones. You missed your bus that night because you didn't want to leave the amputee in R-36, who was crying and holding on to your arm.

I'd been hoping for a chance to talk to you."

In spite of my reluctance, I enjoyed the evening. The thought was always in my mind ... why can't I be doing some of these things with Harold? He just got back from spending a short leave in Honolulu, pretty much alone—I guess. Actually, I would rather he had someone with whom he could spend a leave. I'd be jealous of that person, but I can't bear that he is so lonely. I know his mind is on what's coming up, and I'm sure he wonders if he'll ever see his family and loved ones again. Or if he'll ever be able to do the things he loves to do, like hike in the mountains, much less marry and have children.

29 JULY 1945. CENSORED

Hi Sparky Darlin',

As you see, since this letter reached Cedar City, I received your happy letter of 24 July yesterday. I guess your happiness lent it wings, for that's a bit quicker than normal.

I was happy to receive both items of good news, and I know that right now you must be in seventh heaven. And if you're there, where must Dick be! It must be an utterly glorious feeling for a man to come home to his wife and beautiful little daughter. Please give him my best regards.

The news concerning Ham's promotion was great also. I knew he was limited to a great extent as flight officer, and he was really doing a man-sized job. Send him my congratulations.

Gad, Carmen, but you do hit upon the things I yearn for— beach parties, barbecues, horseback riding, and all the. rest. I do a bit of dreaming, too, you know, now and again. What a great day it will be when this is all over! I'm just wondering now how long it's going to take me to get out of this outfit once the

war is over. Too damned long, I'm afraid. However, I'm not com-
plaining, and there's no outfit in the world I'd rather be with as
long as the war continues. But when it's over—someone else is
welcome to my "leaves" here.

Incidentally, that surely sounded like a wonderful home you
visited in Beverly Hills. That sounds like my kind of house exactly. I'm not interested in "spindly-legged or modernistic" furniture either. I'd surely like to see that home. And, while we're
on the subject of homes, I just learned that my parents have
moved again! It seems they bought two houses in Phoenix and
had the one they liked most entirely remodeled while living in
the other. Burt's and Harriet's letters have been full of the
"new" home, and it really sounds attractive. Give my very best
to all your family—and have fun. Well, Carmen, time to secure.
Love, Harold

There's that damn "have fun" again. That means he knows
he's going into combat. That upsets me so! This is the first time
he's said he wanted to get out of the Corps when the war was
over, but true to form, he doesn't complain.

5 AUGUST 1945. CENSORED

Dearest Carmen,

I received your letter of 31 July this afternoon, and before
I opened it, I noticed it was from Cedar City. Gad, darling, I was
so happy for you. I know how wonderful it must have been for
you to have gone home. That, in itself, would have been great,
but for Dick to have been there, too, must have made the
homecoming utterly super! I wish so much I could have been
there, appropriate or no, to ride out to Dick's land and to go to
the ranch with you. I know you'll be back in L.A. before you receive this (since I'm going to send this to L.A.) but I really wish
you'd wish Dick my best. I'd really like to meet that guy—and
fully plan to some day!

Carmen, darling, even from here, I can see that these first

two pages are barely discernible—or legible. About two hours ago, some of the enlisted men in the Supply Section came after me. They were having a party and wanted me to sit in for a while. Good bunch of men! Obviously, I did, and as a consequence I'm a little tight—and tight I become a bit more relaxed and confidential. And confidentially—between us two, I have my billfold picture of you out before me—and gad, Sparky darling, how I wish I were with you right now!! Do you remember the picture you sent me in that billfold? It's really good! Wish I had my fingers entwined in that soft auburn hair right now. Suppose by my sober standard I'm maudlin, or nearly so, right now, but, fully sober, I'm normally too reserved to be myself. At any rate, Carmen darling, when next you see me, you'll have an opportunity to see me both ways and can choose for yourself.

Good night, darling, and I'll be seein' you. Love, Hap

All his mail has to be censored, even though he's on the censoring board himself. He's always told me he wasn't going to write letters like the Swabbys' (sailors)—cheap drivel, he called it. This letter is barely readable in spots ... a change from his large, pristine penmanship. I know he's *really* homesick and discouraged. I believe he misses me, as I do him.

I wonder if it's possible that he cares for me as much as I do for him.

In 1940 President Roosevelt and Prime Minister Churchill agree to pool the knowledge of Great Britain and the United States for the development of an atomic bomb, which President Truman calls "The battle of the Laboratories."

From then until August 6, 1945, this effort is the world's best-kept secret despite the fact that, at one time, 125,000 persons are involved in extracting uranium and producing the other essentials required for what scientists call "atomic fission." It is the scientists of the United States, Great Britain, and Canada who make the bomb possible.

Shortly before 9 o'clock on a Monday morning, residents

of the city and army base of Hiroshima rush to air-raid shelters when two B-29 bombers fly overhead. The planes circle Hiroshima two or three times, then move away. The "all-clear" sounds. The Japanese don't know that those two planes are checking the weather, visibility, wind, and other data for a third B-29, which appears as the people begin to go about their business.

At 9:15 A.M. a parachute drops from the bomb bay of the third B-29. At its end is a bomb casing holding a small explosive charge. At about 1,500 feet from the ground, it is as if the world has suddenly come to an end. A tremendous flash, like a ball of fire, illuminates everything for scores of miles around. It is visible from the air 170 miles away. Then a funnel of smoke, dust, fire, and color mount like a waterspout up, up, up ever higher until the pillar of boiling dust has reached the stratosphere. In two minutes, the head is 40,000 feet above the ground and still rising.

In spite of the fact that, in a split second, 60 percent of Hiroshima has been wiped off the map, Japan refuses to surrender. Three days later the second atomic bomb falls on Nagasaki. It is more powerful than the first bomb, and in the center of the area where it hit, a vacuum is created—there are no signs of any building. Everything has vanished.

The final blow for Japan is the entrance of Russia into the Pacific War, as a result of President Truman's efforts at Potsdam. On August 8, Russia's Ambassador Sato declares war against Japan, and on August 9, the Red Army sweeps into Manchuria. Japan has no choice but to surrender.

Great Britain and the United States reluctantly unleashed the bomb against Japan to shorten the war and save tens of thousands of American and British lives—and certainly Japanese lives as well. Had they known the true extent of Japan's arsenal of men and weapons, and the truth of their treatment of prisoners of war, they would have been far less reluctant to use that technology.

CHAPTER 12

An Uneasy Peace

On August 10, the same day Russia enters the war, Japan asks for peace, but with a proviso that the emperor will be allowed to retain his powers. The Allies reply to the offer, insisting that the emperor must take orders from the victorious powers.

On August 12, a false radio flash over American networks sets off a premature celebration around the world. Three days later, Japan communicates acceptance of the peace terms, and Emperor Hirohito delivers an imperial directive announcing Japan's defeat.

Dear Diary,

I was at work when the radio announced Japan had surrendered to the Allies. The city went crazy. Mr. Schwartzmann immediately closed the store and activated the security systems. He left in the taxi, which took him home every night while the rest of us finished our closing chores. It was my job to balance the NCR tapes.

By the time we finished, Broadway was a teeming mass of humanity. Streetcars were stalled, with no operators in sight. There were no taxis, and pedestrians found it difficult to get around stalled and abandoned vehicles. Horns were honking, sirens blared, and paper fragments dropped from office windows.

Everyone was in a frenzy. Some couples were kissing or more intimately expressing their jubilation over the end of the war. Men in uniform were so overjoyed they hugged each other and anyone else they could grab. Some of the young women appeared to be trying to fend off the attentions of overly exuberant men taking advantage of the hysteria. We didn't like what we saw, so Irys and I decided to stay in the store for the night rather than take our chances on the street. Then the phone rang; it was our friend Helen suggesting we risk walking the block and a half to her office. As a receptionist in the penthouse office of the J. Baxter Co. building, she felt it was the safest place in the area. She assured us the doorman would be downstairs to let us in.

We made it, a bit roughed up, but when we took the elevator to the top floor it was like being in another world ... quiet, luxurious, and safe. Mr. Baxter, Jr., came out of his office, greeted us warmly and invited us to stay as long as we wanted to. There was a bedroom in the event we must spend the night. He showed us a refrigerator filled with food, opened the bar with a flourish, and mixed a drink for us. We stayed until 2:00 A.M., when the streetcars started running again.

Sleep was impossible that night. With Dick already home, all I could think about was Harold and my brother Ham. I had to pinch myself to know I was awake and not dreaming. I can't even imagine what it would be like to see them and for life to be normal once again. I felt light as a feather, like a heavy shell had been lifted from my entire body ... surely now the men I love will be sent home.

The next day, downtown Los Angeles was still a mess, but I was expected to show up for work. Mr. Schwartzmann decided to close early when it became obvious there would be few customers. I, for one, was too excited to concentrate on work.

That evening I called home and talked to my mom and dad; then the phone rang, and it was Paul Bradford calling.

"Carmen, I've been thinking about you today and know how happy you must be. I would like to take you to dinner Saturday to celebrate."

I accepted his invitation, and Saturday we went to the same

private club in the city. He ordered champagne and proposed a toast to the future. I had never tasted champagne before ... it gave me the giggles. I really believe he meant it when he said there were no strings attached to our friendship. Why shouldn't it be possible for a man and woman to be friends or am I kidding myself?

"I have a twofold question for you, Carmen. Are you engaged to your marine, and do you expect him to come home soon?"

"No, we're not engaged. I've seen him only once in five years, as he's been out of the country and in combat for a long time. I don't think my feelings for him have changed ... and from his letters, it appears his have not, either. I guess time will tell. As for coming home soon ... I have no idea. He's a career marine ... it's possible enlistees and draftees will be sent home first."

"You and he certainly deserve the best life has to offer. In the meantime, I trust you won't cross me off your list until you see him and make a decision.

When I tried to tell him I don't want to waste his time, he brushed me off and said the time we spend together is not, in his opinion, wasted.

After dinner, we danced to an orchestra brought in for a victory celebration. I hadn't danced for a long time and was pleased when Paul turned out to be a darn good dancer. I guess that's to be expected of someone who played in a dance band.

I was still feeling giggly from the excitement of the war news, champagne, and the fun of dancing. At first the orchestra played tunes popular with the more dignified guests, then, with a roll on the drums and a crash of the cymbals, erupted into a brisk rendition of "Alexander's Ragtime Band." Without a moment's hesitation, Paul adjusted to the new beat and we were off! I felt like I was back in college, dancing my heart out. When the tune ended, the lights dimmed and "That Old Feeling," a favorite of mine and Harold's, was the final straw. Tears welled up in my eyes, and I welcomed being held close so no one could see. I'm forgetting we're just friends and he shouldn't be holding me so close. I'm not used to champagne.

When we got back to the apartment, I invited him to come in and meet my roommates. They were charmed ... and envious.

I worried I'd given him more encouragement than I intended.

---

18 AUGUST 1945

Dearest Carmen,

Surely was great to hear of your visit home and all the things you did. I know how wonderful it must have been for you. I can visualize so much of that country and love it so well! When you spoke of flying over Zion Canyon, I almost ached. It'll be a great day for me when I can go puffing up East Rim Trail again. The last time I climbed that trail was in the spring of 1940—in the moonlight. Got back to camp about 0400. What a beautiful, gorgeous night that was!

No, Sparky, I really do not have time for any reading yet. It's quite apparent to you, I'm sure, that I don't even have the time to do justice to my correspondence to you—and you rate at the top of the list with my family. Our training schedule has not lightened one iota, nor does there seem to be any indication that it will do so in the near future. In fact, I should not be surprised if things actually tightened down a bit. Have spent a great deal of the last two months in the field, and just got in this evening from another session.

Was relieved to learn from your letter of 10 August that my letter of the 5th didn't get me "in dutch." And I'm glad you are letting your hair grow. I like long hair.

Well, for the war—Carmen darlin', I swear I am not a pessimist! Yet in the midst of all this hilarity, I sit untouched—even subdued—for I'm afraid we may have stopped too soon. Statesmanship—American statesmanship—has never gained anything for this country. In every dealing with foreign powers, we, the businessmen, the trailblazers, always seem to come out on the short end of the deal. I sincerely hope that this time our diplomats wrest from Japan all that she should pay for the destruction she has caused.

I'm sure you won't misunderstand me. I hate this war, and I find little attractive in this life I'm living. I want this war to be over. But, having come this far and given up so much in time, lives, and material goods, I feel we should have continued until we made absolutely certain Japan would never again, in our time, be able to mass a war machine such as the one she launched against us in 1941. I disagree violently with our use of the "Atomic Bomb"—as we used it! If it is the weapon propagandists would have us believe, I firmly believe we should have used it to the fullest extent of our ability and smashed and smashed and smashed Japan until she groveled for mercy! She is a nation utterly without honor, and I'm sure she would have had no compunction about using such a weapon on us. Instead, we slap her on the wrist; ask her to quit; then slap her on the wrist again. So help me, with our weak policies, we shouldn't be allowed to play at war with the rest of the nations of the world! War is something to be pursued viciously, with all the weapons at your disposal! There is no such thing as civilized warfare! All one has to do to realize that is to look over row upon row upon row of twisted, burned, mangled bodies of marines lying upon a stinking Iwo beach waiting for burial. Ten thousand enemy lives are not worth one marine life. For they were the aggressors; and the civilians were just as guilty as the military, for they countenanced and supported the conflict wholeheartedly.

Well, Sparky, I seem to have gotten a bit wound up, but that's the way I feel about the whole thing. I most certainly do not blame the folks back home for being jubilant over the end of the war. I realize what a tremendous strain they have undergone all this time, worrying about their loved ones out here. For them, I'm happy. And, if things come out the way our stateside dreamers plan, I'll be just very doggone happy for myself.

As for coming home in the very near future—I'm afraid that's out. We have no dope, of course, but it looks to me as if we still have a pretty fair-sized job to do out here yet in getting the word to some of the Jap outposts and policing enemy territories. However, just bet your lucky stars that as soon as they slack up on the reins, this lad is homeward bound! There goes "Taps" right now, darlin', and the day starts early in the morning, so guess I'd better secure. "Night." Love, Harold

26 AUGUST, 1945. CENSORED

Hi Sparky darlin',

This is not even a feeble attempt to answer your last letters. I'm bound for the field for another five days in the morning, though, and just had to get a note off to you before we went, I'll save your letters to answer on my return, but wanted you to know the cause of the delay.

Glad to get all the good dope on stateside happenings and can surely understand all the elation there. Hasn't affected our work much here as yet, but guess it soon will—I hope. Well, darling, it's long after taps and I have a long march ahead of me in the morning. Night, Carmen. Love, Harold

---

The Japanese delegation flies into Ie Shima, where they are transferred to an American plane, then flown to Manila to receive instructions from General MacArthur. Prior to their arrival, the entire island is searched for men well over six feet to be the honor guards. Although there are higher-ranking officers on Okinawa, MacArthur brings in a 6'7" brigadier general to meet the Japanese and transfer them to the American plane. The guards are furnished new uniforms and told not to shake hands. The small-statured Japanese look like children walking between the tall guards and the very tall general, which was MacArthur's intent.

September 2, 1945, the Japanese premier and military leaders sign formal surrender documents onboard the battleship USS *Missouri* in Tokyo Bay.

In the days following surrender, Second Lieutenant Leigh's squadron of C-47s are among those that fly in the initial occupation troops. Since Leigh is the liaison for the squadron, he goes in with the first flight.

They also fly inspection and occupation troops to various places in Japan and transport American prisoners of war back to Atsugi, where those able can be flown to Manila for medical treatment and then to the United States.

Dear Diary,

It's been two weeks since V.J. Day, when Irys and I spent most of the night in the J. Baxter Penthouse. Helen called today to say Mr. Baxter wants to interview me for her job. Her marine is on his way home, and she has given notice. I've heard from Harold that he doesn't expect to be sent home in the immediate future, so I agreed to the interview.

Mr. Baxter is the most sophisticated man I have ever met, with the possible exception of Paul Bradford. He didn't ask for references, saying Helen's recommendation was all he needed. He asked what my salary was at Rhodes. When I told him, he smiled and assured me, "we can do MUCH better than that," all the while patting my knee. He expected an immediate answer, but when I told him I wanted to give enough notice for my replacement to be found ... he was instantly charming and, still patting my knee, "By all means, take your time."

I have misgivings ... a feeling I might be getting in over my head. I'm thinking about it.

In fact, that experience has caused me to think of another area where I might be getting in over my head. I'm still concerned about my last evening with Paul Bradford. I fear I might have given him a wrong impression. I'm considering quitting at the Rehab Center. They won't need me now the war is over. As long as I'm there, seeing him every week, it will be more difficult to maintain a casual friendship with him. I enjoy his companionship and the attention he gives me, but considering my feelings for Harold, I realize I'm not being fair to Paul. From things he says, I get the impression he'd like to marry and have a family. If that's true, he should be devoting his time to someone with whom he might have a future.

---

3 SEPTEMBER 1945. CENSORED

Dearest Carmen,

Time at last for a fairly decent letter! Sorry it has been so long delayed, but our training has continued as before—and long periods of "boondocking" are not conducive to letter writing.

I was sorry after I had written my last letter that I had been so frank about my views, for I fear they may have been depressing, and you all surely do rate a celebration! But I assure you I'm not a pessimist! It is simply that I refuse to believe things quite so rosy as the correspondents and politicians would have us believe. However, from the way things are going at present, it looks as if I may have been a shade too dubious. Well, time will tell, and in the meantime we may as well enjoy our hard-won peace. And, darling, in spite of the sour notes of my letter, I enjoyed your description of the victory celebration.

Say, Sparky, how about the picture of that dress—and you—you promised me? I'm waitin'. And, incidentally, where did you find out they call me "Hap" in the service? And, not so incidentally, that deal about the J. Baxter Co. does sound interesting.

As for myself, things look somewhat brighter—although all's still pure guesswork. Still have no idea how long it will take for a regular officer to obtain his release, but I think there's a good chance of my coming stateside, at least well before the end of the other 14 months I had expected to spend out here this time. However, I repeat, this is all surmise, and the only way we ever know is to actually receive orders.

So—again I wait. Goodnight, Carmen. Love, Harold

14 SEPTEMBER 1945

Dearest Carmen,

How goes all with you tonight? Things look pretty good from here. Don't recall whether I told you my brother-in-law is to be released shortly. I'm overjoyed at the thought he and Harriet can resume a normal life. Burt is going into the insurance business with Father, so guess when Jim and I return it will really be quite the family affair. I do hope that Ham, too, will soon be home. What is he going to do? The flying bug hasn't bitten him so badly he'll want to stay in, has it?

Well, Sparky, it appears we may not be over here as long as I had predicted. There's no definite dope as yet, but indications are numerous that we may move ere long. And, since I doubt they need us further out, I presume they'll send us stateside. Time alone will tell, but if it gives the wrong answer, we'll be a bunch of sad sacks!

Well, goodnight, darlin'. Enough guessing for tonight—but more later. Love, Harold

---

SEPTEMBER 22, 1945

Hi, Sparky darlin',

Thanks for your letter of the 16th. It was great to learn that Ham expects to be home by Christmas.

Well, Carmen, we found out today what the basis for return of 4th Mar Div personnel to the States was to be—and I don't qualify. One must have had at least 15 months out of the States on *this* tour of duty in order to return with the Division, so my 38 months don't stack up to much ... have been out only 11 months this time. Oh, well, just part of the system, I guess. I hadn't really counted on going back so soon, so am not too disappointed. However, any delay in my return to the States—and consequent "rebirth"—now that the war is over, I'm going to find more than a bit irksome. Enough for now. As ever, Harold

---

Dear Diary,

I'm devastated. This is the first time in five years I detect real depression in his letters. And there's that "As ever" again ... I wonder what it means *now*! I feel sorry for him—and myself.

I was so sure from his last two letters he'd be coming home, and was not surprised he's thinking of resigning his commission and going into business with his family. So I called Mr. Baxter and declined his offer of a job and also quit volunteer work at the Rehab Center. Looks like I was too hasty ... maybe I should have accepted Mr. Baxter's offer, and continued at the center, where I feel useful.

Doris and I have to start looking for another apartment soon. We're losing Alice and Ellen and can't afford this big place. At this rate, I may be in L.A. until HELL FREEZES OVER!

28 SEPTEMBER 1945. CENSORED

Dearest Carmen,

Today the word came out, and there's no more guess-work—as far as I'm concerned, at least. As of 1 October, I'll take over as "exec" of an MP battalion which is forming up to go west. I know our destination, and it should be interesting. Can't give you the scoop on that, however, until we arrive there.

All of the "old men" of the original 4th Mar Div will embark very shortly for return to the States, along with all the reserve officers with sufficient points for discharge. Surely wish I had the little old "R" behind my name, for I have almost twice as many points as I need. Ho hum!

Sounds as if you are getting ambitious in your reading. When we get organized "out west," I hope I'll have time for some serious reading. Noticed in your last letter you have a yen for an ocean voyage. Guess I'm due for another within ten days or so. I've really learned to love the sea, and I'm always glad to get under way.

Well, enough for now, Sparky. Time to turn in, days are hectic now we're in the midst of reorganization. Love, Harold

Dear Diary,

How can he be so good-natured after all this time? For the last three years, every time he's expected to be sent to Camp Pendleton near Los Angeles, there's been a last-minute change. I'd feel better if he'd rant and rave and cuss a blue streak. At least he won't be in any more combat, although there's still danger from the enemy. Some of the Japanese soldiers are in outlying islands, dug into caves, and don't even know the war is over.

I almost wish I hadn't given notice at the center, but it's too late now. This is my last day as a regular. I made a point of visiting the patients I've worked with, especially David, the young amputee in R-36. He lost both legs when he stepped on a land mine. I assured him I would still be substituting and promised not to forget him.

Near the end of the day, the floor nurse handed me a note from Paul asking me to stop in his office when my shift ended.

"Well, Carmen, what's this I hear about you leaving us? Is your young man coming home?"

"I intended to tell you before I left today if you had time to talk to me. No, I don't think Harold will be home right away. I'm hoping to make some trips to Utah to see my brothers soon, so I won't have all my Saturdays available. I have been put on the substitute volunteer list."

He glanced at his nurse, whose desk is within earshot. She's got a case on him and is very possessive ... always appears to be curious about what we have to say to each other.

"I'll walk you to the bus, if you don't mind." Instead he escorted me to the doctors' lounge, where we could be alone.

"I hope you know how much I enjoyed being with you last Saturday. You're some kind of a dancer for sure."

"So are you. Every woman in the room wanted to dance with you."

"Carmen, I'm going to be out of town for at least the next two weeks. My aunt and uncle want me to go to Hawaii with them to visit a grave, at Punch Bowl cemetery, believed to be that of their son. Positive identification is not possible, but they have accepted the likelihood that it is his.

"My cousin and I are the same age. His parents hoped he'd go to medical school when I did, but he wanted to have a career in the navy. Now I'm the only family they have. I will call you as soon as I return. Incidentally, my aunt Eleanor asks about you every time I see her. She wants me to bring you out to see them soon. I promised her I would."

I'm glad Paul's going to be away for a while. It's possible he's interested in someone else and would like to make a graceful exit. Since I won't be at the center every week, he won't have to be concerned about me.

CHAPTER 13

Homeward Bound?

Dear Diary,

Everybody I know is coming home now that the war is over... everyone but Harold. Sometimes I wonder if the good Lord is trying to tell me something. Am I crazy to hang on to a dream that perhaps never was reality? I've been lucky to know some very good men in my life. First there was Butch—a real gem. Then several other really nice guys in the years since. Always when the chips were down, I found myself unable to grab the brass ring because Harold wasn't holding it. When he does come home ... if he ever does ... will we even know each other?

At least Dick and some of my cousins are home. Ham is safe so far and expects to come home soon. Cousins Leigh Lunt and Francis Betenson haven't been found; both are believed to be prisoners of the Germans.

4 OCTOBER 1945

Dearest Carmen,

Just a line, for we're really swamped trying to get this new MP battalion organized and equipped. Trying to get all gear crated at the same time, for we're soon to load to go west.

Looks as if it's going to be a good outfit. As I told you, since I have to stay out, I'm glad to be going with this outfit.

Received your disappointed letter of the 28th. I, too, was disappointed, but not surprised. Anyway, the longer they keep me in this outfit, the more determined I become to withdraw as soon as I can.

You asked how many points I had. I have 113, but they don't count for regulars. All reserves with 60 points are going home with division. Regulars with 15 months out this time are going home. I had 38 months in all, but only 11 this time, so I don't qualify there, either. Ho hum! Guess there's no alternative. Do another year and I can come home. I'm used to it by now. Nothing bothers me very much.

As I may have told you, my boss is a great guy, and there are compensations for being exec of this outfit. A year or so of this isn't going to strain me too much.

Well, good night, Sparky darlin'. Love, Hap
P.S. New address is: 8th Military Police Battalion (prov)
Fleet Marine Forces,Pacific, c/o fleet Post Office,
San Francisco, Calif.

7 Nov. 1945
Dearest Carmen,

About to finish another long hop. The day after tomorrow brings us to Okinawa. What a hectic month the past one has been, trying to form this battalion, equip it, and prepare all for shipment. By the time we came aboard a week ago Monday, I was really ready for a rest.

We've had a pretty nice trip, so far. This ship, a converted hospital ship, rolls heavily, and we've had quite a few sick men and officers, but to me it has been great to get back to sea. I love it!

Tonight, dusk will find us only 150 miles north of Iwo Jima, which I have no yen ever to gaze upon again. Crossed the International Date Line for the 11th time last Friday. Do have a yen to cross that one more time—and only one. After that, I plan to confine my activities to state lines.

The mail situation in this outfit is really desperate. We have not received one solitary scrap of mail since our activation almost six weeks ago. Apparently, all our mail was sent directly to Okinawa, while we were sitting restlessly on Maui. If we don't find a whole carload of mail awaiting us here, though, we're going to have a lot of disappointed men on our hands.

What's the latest new from home, Sparky? How's Jackie, where's Ham? I have no idea how things are going in Phoenix.

Hope I find all the answers in the mail.

More soon from "Oky." Love, Hap

Paul is back from Hawaii. He wants a date for this coming Saturday, but my roommates and I have planned a little party on the weekend for some friends here in the apartment house. We've included Old Doc, who, of all things, just got engaged to be married . . . will wonders never cease! His fiancée doesn't live in L.A., so he didn't accept for her. I have to admit Doc has been good to us in spite of being such a pill at times. Thankfully, we've all been fast enough on our feet to keep from being alone with him, so all is well. He's been a challenge! We'll miss him.

I don't think Paul will have much in common with the other guests, but I invited him and, to my surprise, he accepted. He'll spend the night in a hotel close by so we can have some time together the next day.

Actually, the evening turned out well. Doris and Alice are really great cooks. The food was excellent, and Ellen and I did our best to be efficient waitresses. Paul went out of his way to be charming. Doc behaved himself for a change. Being engaged is good for him.

This morning, Paul and I had brunch at the Ambassador. He filled me in on his trip to Hawaii and asked what the latest word is on Harold.

"He's been sent to Okinawa as exec of an MP battalion. It will likely be a year before that tour of duty will end. I promised him a current picture, but don't know a good photographer in Los Angeles. Do you have a suggestion? I promised him I'd send it for Christmas."

"Yes, I do ... the Jerome Kern studio in Hollywood. It is excellent. They owe me a favor, and I'll take you there during lunch hour this week. You name the day.

"I miss seeing you at the center, Carmen. I'm determined not to lose track of you, in spite of this change in your life."

I miss being there, but I need to be free to go home when my brothers are released from service. I must say, you were the life of the party last night. My roommates fell for you and, I think Old Doc was jealous of the attention you got from the ladies.

"I enjoyed meeting your friends, especially Doc. He is a character. I think he gets a kick out of shocking people, but I found him interesting. We have some things in common, though where you are concerned, we differ.

"I can't see that you two are alike in any way, Paul."

"I recall you telling me what Doc said when you thanked him for calling the police after that army captain went berserk at your apartment. He told you he did it because if anyone was going to seduce you, he'd rather it would be him. In my case I want you to know, I don't want to seduce you ... I'm thinking more along the lines of a permanent relationship."

It was embarrassing ... I wondered, is he serious? I didn't know what to say. "Gosh, Paul, you barely know me."

"I know you well enough to know what I want."

I tried to change the subject, but he was persistent.

"There is a favor I'd like to ask of you. When your marine comes home and you make a decision, will you promise me you will pick up the phone and give me a call? All you need to say is: 'I'm engaged' ... or, 'I'm not engaged.' In the meantime, I want to spend as much time with you as our schedules will permit ... promise me you will make that call."

The following Friday, I was able to arrange a long lunch hour. Paul made the appointment and picked me up for the photo shoot. I was flabbergasted when I saw the studio. It was very ritzy and obviously patronized by the movie stars whose pictures covered the walls.

"Paul, I don't think I can afford to have my picture taken here."

Now, Carmen, I told you the owner owed me a favor. It will not be expensive at all, and you'll get a first-rate picture."

"Paul, I want to pay for this. It is Harold's Christmas present."

The picture was flattering. In fact, I couldn't believe it was me, and Paul insisted the charge was a measly $10.00.

---

13 NOVEMBER, 1945. BATEN KO, OKINAWA

Mornin', Sparky Darlin',

Arrived in Buckner Bay on the 9th and unloaded our battalion the afternoon and night of the 10th. Had to unload in the stream instead of alongside a dock. Am damned glad that's over.

This island appears to be very attractive from what I've seen of it. We have two camps twenty-five miles apart assigned to us, and our living conditions are good. Our men are all living in tents at present, but we expect to get them into Quonset huts before winter sets in. The colonel and I are quartered in a nice private Quonset, with refrigerator, and are getting shaken down for a good tour of duty. At any rate, it's the best living either of us has seen for a year. Guess even at that it would look pretty rugged to you.

Our quarters are up on the hillside overlooking Buckner Bay, and the view is lovely. Also visible from our quarters are about 100 craft beached or sunk by the recent typhoon. The view really is beautiful at night, though, with all the ships lighted in the harbor and with darkness covering N.O.B. (noncommissioned officers barracks)

Surely was great to get ashore, Carmen, and receive our backlog of mail, the first in seven weeks. Yesterday and today, I've received five October letters from you. I was glad to learn Jackson had called you and overjoyed to receive his wedding announcement yesterday. That's one I would like to attend, and today's the day, isn't it?

Dick Jackson is a sergeant who has worked with Harold since he was attached to the 4th Marine Division. Dick qualified to come home with the division and is in L.A. getting ready to marry. Harold has recommended Dick to his father, who is developing a sales force for his new agency in Phoenix.

Don't know what I'm going to do for their wedding present, as I understand all the villages on the island are absolutely demolished and all the villagers are destitute. I'll have a quick look around here before I decide. May ask you to do my shopping for me, since I presume you have met Blanche. How about it?

Thanks for the picture of your brother Dick. And speaking of pictures, I'll be looking forward to that picture of your new suit—and you.

Yes, Carmen, it appears I'll have some time for reading on this job. I have no particular requests, other than *Fountainhead*. I place myself in your good hands.

Had a bit of a close call yesterday while returning from our north camp at Lengan. Had to stop for a traffic jam, and while I was stopped, a 5-ton wrecker hit me from the rear and completely demolished my jeep. Had one of my lieutenants with me. We were both in good shape today, however, and consider ourselves damned lucky.

Say, Sparky darlin', this Armed Forces Radio Station here (WXLH) is the real thing. No commercials—just good music and entertainment all day long. In fact, it's just what stateside stations should be. Right now they're playing "Amapolo." Remember that one? I'll bet you do. Those college dances were so much fun! They just played "Sentimental Journey."

Well, darling, guess this is about enough for one time. Love, Hap   P.S. Just learned Jim is now in Heidelberg.

Well if that isn't ironic. Harold goes through a suicide mission, Battle of the Savo Sea, and Iwo Jima in the Pacific; the opening of the Mediterranean front; surrender of the Italians at Taranto; and several operations in New Guinea without a scratch, then he almost gets hurt, or worse, sitting in a jeep caught in a traffic jam. Thank goodness he's all right.

There was lots of excitement in our neighborhood this weekend. The survivors of the Bataan Death March and other Japanese prisoners of war are being brought home. Those from southern California are arriving at MacArthur Park just across the street from our apartment house. The physically able will be met there by their family and friends. This is such an historic event, we decided to go to the park.

The evening of August 9, 1945, an event similar to others occurring in prison camps all over Japan, takes place. A lieutenant colonel and six Japanese American *Neise* sergeants bail out of a B-24 into a cabbage patch next door to a prison camp housing survivors of the Bataan Death March. They spend the night in Mukden and the next morning are brought to the camp, where they bring the prisoners up to date on what is going on in the world and tell them about the dropping of the atomic bombs.

The following day, the Russians arrive and, for the first time since their capture, the prisoners are given everything they ask for and are told they will be on their way home as soon as possible

They are taken out of Japan, into Russian territory. Two weeks later, the prisoners are taken, via the Trans-Siberian Railway, to a waiting American hospital ship. Here the prisoners see American sailors, doctors, and nurses in white uniforms and finally realize their prison-camp days are over.

Along with other prisoners being liberated, they are transported to the Philippines by boat and from there by ship or in B-24s to the United States. In San Francisco, the sick and badly injured are taken to Letterman's General Hospital. The ablebodied are then taken to receiving areas as near to their homes as possible.

I feel fortunate I could witness the happiness of this reunion. These men have suffered starvation, torture, and ill treatment, in some cases for five years. They are unbelievably thin, many have no hair at all on their heads, and their eyes look too large for their shrunken faces. Still, I've never seen such happiness on the faces of human beings in all my life. If these are the able-bodied ones, what shape must the others be in?

I noticed a man I thought was looking at me. I stared back at him because he looked familiar. I never was able to find out anything more about Art Culver after my letters came back marked "Missing." One reason I wanted to come here today was because I wondered if, after he was shot down, he'd been captured by the Japanese. His family lives in Arcadia, so if that were the case and he was alive, he would be brought to this receiving point ... unless he's so ill he had to be taken to a hospital. This man's face haunts me, and the way he looked at me made me wonder. Could it be Art Culver? Maybe!

BATEN KO, OKINAWA
28 NOVEMBER 1945

Evenin', Sparky darlin',

Really feel in the mood to answer four of your sweet letters tonight as I sit here listening to the wonderful music of the Cleveland orchestra. Gad, but it is lovely!

Surely enjoyed your account of Dick's and Blanche's wedding. I was glad to hear of Bob's and Helen's wedding also. They too, must be hilariously happy. And, yes, I do know Rome. I like those rebel boys. Just finished a letter to Rome, for he's another I plan to keep track of.

Carmen, I notice from your letter of the 19th that you still haven't received any mail from me. Had supposed the service better in that direction. I wrote you aboard before we disembarked here and have written several since. Guess it will break through eventually. Notice it's still well-fouled-up out here, for yesterday I received your letters of the 1st and 19th. A slight discrepancy, wouldn't you say?

With Ham coming home soon and Jackie progressing well, it looks like a merry Christmas for the Leighs, after all.

Well, darlin', guess I'll secure for tonight. Am getting pretty sleepy. I'm enclosing—at long last—a snapshot, taken in our club here on Okinawa. It is essentially the truth. Night, honey, Hap

P.S. heard from John Hall today. His ship just left Long Beach on the "Magic Carpet" run to New Caledonia. Tried to find you but failed; so I sent him your address, as he expects to be back in around the first of the year. H

BATEN KO, "OKIE." 3 DECEMBER 1945

Hi, Sparky Darlin',

If this turns out to be more illegible than usual, it's because we (the Col. and I) have just acquired a couch (of sorts) and I am treating myself to the unaccustomed luxury of lying here— sipping on a good, cold beer, to write this letter. Already I can see it doesn't look very clear—but here I stay. It'd take about 5 lbs. of c-2 to move me from here, and 2 lbs. does a pretty terrific job on a pillbox!

Received my first letter from Dick Jackson today—his letter of *23 October!* Talk about stinking mail service. And, as if that weren't enough, we just found out tonight that Cincpack has originated a dispatch sending our mail to Nagasaki, Japan—of all places—and that the bulk of our mail for the past 15 days has already gone there. We are really whizzed off—but it does explain our scanty recent mail. I'm really quite disgusted over such incompetence.

Thanks, Carmen, for consenting to do my shopping for Dick and Blanche. Will try to get over and draw some money tomorrow, and if I can make it, I'll enclose a money order for their wedding gift in this letter. Night and Love, Hap

10 DECEMBER 1945

Well, Sparky,

The departure of this note leaves me more than a bit chagrined, for, as you've noted, I started it a week ago. I put off mailing it until I could draw money, and since we have to go halfway up the island, I couldn't get away long enough to make the trip until yesterday.

In the meantime, I've received two more of your wonderful letters, as well as the copy of Tolstoy. Thanks so much for all three. I've wanted to read that book for some time. Glad to hear your Thanksgiving dinner was such a huge success, but I anticipated it would be.

Well, Carmen darlin', it's a bit after midnight, and I have to be on deck bright and early in the morning to relieve our duty officers and try a deck court, so I'm off to bed. Just couldn't wait another day to get this letter off, though. Love, Hap

BATEN KO. 23 DECEMBER 1945

Dearest Carmen,

Just this morning I received your letter of 9 Dec. Our mail service for the past three weeks has been simply "stinking." In fact, I've had only one letter from home since we left Maui. Your letters do come through better than that, thank God!

Yes, Sparky, I have received both of the books you sent, and I've started *Fountainhead*. Like it immensely as far as I've gone. Thanks for them also. You say you've sent the picture you promised me. It hasn't come yet. I ache to see your face. Oh, well, it will eventually come through.

Don't believe I've mentioned our radio service here on Okinawa. It is by far the most satisfactory station to which I've ever listened. It is an Armed Forces station, and its programs are utterly devoid of those disgusting commercials. They consist of recordings (both classical and popular), news and rebroadcasts of important or popular stateside broadcasts. At present I'm listening to the "Hour of Charm." Christmas carols, of course, and they really sound lovely. Don't believe there is actually such a thing as Christmas out here. One just doesn't get the feeling. Was very glad to hear you pulled through the siege of sickness at the apartment, without yourself falling prey. This is really your busy season, isn't it?

I'm enclosing a couple of snapshots of possible interest. These are shots taken at our present camp before and after the October typhoon. I knew it had been disastrous, but I had not realized the full extent of devastation wrought until I saw this pair of pictures. The camp is in fine shape now, but I'd have hated to move in here around the end of October.

Well, Sparky darlin', guess it's high time I secured for tonight. And—Merry Christmas to you all! Love, Hap

Dear Diary,

We hoped Ham would be home for the holidays, but it didn't work out, so I will stay in L.A. and go home when he does make it. With the war over, most everyone is in the mood to make the holidays more festive. I can't seem to get in the spirit now that Harold is even farther away than he was before the war ended.

Seems like everyone wants to have a party. Paul's aunt Eleanor is having one Christmas Day. My roommates and I are planning one for Christmas Eve and, of course, there's a party at the store, which includes the people in several offices close by.

There's something about office parties that turns me off. There are always more men than women, and they are older, obviously, because all of the younger men have been in service. Some of these old guys act like they just fell face down in the cookie jar. Surrounded by younger and, they think, men-hungry young girls, they drink too much and then believe that excuses them for making passes. I'm not in the mood for an office party, but I don't know how to get out of it since the store will be closed early on the last day and I'll already be there. I'm stuck!

I did get a surprise in the mail . . . an invitation to her wedding from Lee Kirby, who has an apartment near the one Leora and I shared on Westmoreland. She's marrying a West Point lieutenant she met at a bar and hopes Irys and I will attend.

She's the girl whose boss pays the rent on her apartment. I like her, though I confess I wonder why a young, attractive, smart girl would do that, but who am I to judge?

The ceremony was at a small wedding chapel. Irys and I were glad we accepted, especially when we saw how few guests were there—several people from Lee's office and a sister of the groom's. Lee's boss gave her away.

I realized Lee doesn't have any family interested enough to be here, and I began to understand her better. Her boss *is* her family. I'm sorry I ever felt critical of her lifestyle and maybe a little superior because I saw myself as a nicer person. Now I see it's just that I'm a more fortunate person. I hope this is a wonderful marriage. Her young man is handsome, well educated, and seems really nice. I'm happy for her.

Our Christmas Eve party will be a "hen party." Alice will soon be going home to Ogden . . . she hopes to marry her Ev before the coming year is over. Ellen has a new job in Studio City. Doris and I will have to look for a new apartment. Some of the girls from downstairs will be leaving to get married. This is the end of an era.

Christmas Day, Paul took me to his aunt Eleanor's for their holiday party. It was elegant and festive. She had several nice presents for me under the tree. When Paul drove me home, we stopped off at a nightclub and danced for a while. I love to dance. He wants me to spend New Year's Eve with him, but I've already accepted a party invitation from girlfriends.

I did accept a date with him for New Year's Day. A lovely holiday bouquet of flowers has been delivered to the apartment from Paul. He really is a nice guy and a good friend.

Harold expects to be on this tour of duty for another year. I am so discouraged and lonely. It will be a long year.

Top: *Harold at his desk, Okinawa;* center, *Harold with friends at the club on Okinawa;* bottom: *At the club.*

Portrait of Carmen taken by Jerome Kern of Hollywood for Harold's Christmas present. He wrote her, "I ache to see your face."

Okinawa—before and after the typhoon.

CHAPTER 14

New Year - Still Alone

Dear Diary,

Thank goodness the holidays will soon be over. I'm tired but lucky I haven't been sick like my roommates. All three got sick during the two weeks before Christmas. We thought we were going to have to cancel our Christmas Eve party for the girls. Mr. Schwartzmann's secretary, Teresa, took sick as well, and I've been doubling up at the store. Haven't heard much from Harold. He says Cincpack goofed and routed their mail by way of Nagasaki, Japan, of all places. He's received some of my letters, but not all, and I haven't had many from him. He's probably been writing more than gets through ... at least, I hope he has. Well, I'll get them sooner or later if he's writing.

I'm a bit concerned about my date with Paul New Year's Day.

I've just found out it will be at his apartment. I assumed there would be other people there, like maybe his aunt and uncle, some of his co-workers and friends. Instead I learned he's planned an afternoon and early evening for just the two of us. He's cooking the dinner. The menu will be a surprise. He promises a fire in the fireplace, dancing to my favorite music, and my favorite wine or champagne. Good grief! I don't have a favorite wine ... I don't know one from the other. I do know champagne goes to my head and I'm leery about drinking much under those circumstances. When I told him that, he laughed.

"Carmen, remember what I told you. I don't want to seduce you and I promise, I'll be a perfect gentleman. Even if you throw yourself at my feet, I WILL RESIST. I'm a good cook, though, and I intend to prove it."

"You're just trying to show me up. You know I don't know how to cook."

"You have other talents. But you are too suspicious of men. We're not all alike, you know. You've been to too many office parties recently and been around "Old Doc" too much.

I'll pick you up at 3:00 P.M. and have you home early. And I'll select the wine."

I've never been to his apartment. It's near his aunt Eleanor's house ... not right in Beverly Hills, but close by. I'm remembering the time we danced, when I had champagne for the first time in my life, I found myself forgetting we were supposed to be just friends. With Harold not coming home now, I've been feeling kind of blue and vulnerable. I've got to get hold of myself and quit feeling like a martyr.

In late October, Officer Henry Leigh has enough points to go home, so is sent from Atsugi, in the Phillipines, to Okinawa for transport to the U.S. Someone has fouled up, and he and his companions sit there for an entire month waiting for a ship. While they are there, a large typhoon passes over the island. In order to protect themselves, the men make their way to a mountain peak where caves were built by the Japanese defenders. The greatest danger is from flying objects such as cots, tents, and poles, and an occasional sheet of tin siding from the Quonset huts that could cut a man in two. The weather station is blown away at 126 miles per hour, and that isn't even the height of the storm.

Finally, a small troop ship comes by on its way to the States. There are no officer accommodations aboard, but they can take it or wait for the next one. Lieutenant Leigh and all the other officers gladly board. They came back via the Great Circle route, which takes them alongside Alaska, then down to

Seattle. There are numerous storms en route, and only the crew is allowed on deck. It takes sixteen days, during which the men are forced to sleep on their stomachs with their arms under the steel railing of the bunks to keep from being thrown out of bed.

They land in Seattle, Washington, mid-December 1945, and are transported to Fort Lewis. That evening, they have dinner in a large central mess hall manned by German prisoners of war. After a year of eating concentrated food, the men find it impossible to eat very much, even though, for the first time in a long while, they have a choice of steaks, pork chops, chicken, beef, and all kinds of fresh fruits and vegetables.

Leigh is informed that an outdated Jim Crow car could be attached to the train for Salt Lake City if there are enough men headed in that direction. It has no heat, is cold and uncomfortable, but it is on his way home. He finally arrives in Salt Lake City and on December 27, 1945, is mustered out of the service. He had gone in the army to get his year of service over before finishing college ... five years and six days later, it was over. He left Okinawa just a few days before Maj. Harold Hiner arrived with the 4th Marine Division.

It's a relief to hear Ham is safe. We believed he was on his way home, but for the last month and a half have not known where he was. His wife Jean met him in Salt Lake.

I've asked Mr. Schwartzmann to give me a few days off after the first of the year so I can go home to see him. It's poor timing, because we're going to be even more short-handed at the store. Irys Hedman's husband, Bud, is on his way home, and she's given notice. That leaves me as the only girl of all those I know who is still waiting for a boyfriend to be released from the service.

Well, today is the first day of 1946 and the day of my date with Paul at his apartment. In spite of some apprehension, I'm looking forward to it. I've been working hard and I'm ready for a little fun. Paul is fun. He makes me laugh, and I'm in the mood for dancing.

It was a beautiful crisp day, the drive to his place a welcome change from my routine bus or streetcar commutes. I was interested in seeing his apartment, curious as to his taste in furnishings, etc. I wondered if I'd see pictures of his lady friends scattered around. I know, from his aunt Eleanor's teasing, he knows plenty of women, but she's not impressed with some of them.

When we entered the apartment; it was filled with wonderful cooking odors which I couldn't identify. The furnishings were tasteful and comfortable. A quick look around didn't reveal much about his social life. No doubt he put those things out of sight. The apartment is small, but the high ceiling made it look larger. The bedroom wing is constructed on one side above the living area, accessible by means of a curved stairway. Downstairs is the spacious living room with a tiny dining area, elegant powder room, and den. I was surprised to see the picture of me taken by the Jerome Kern Studio above his desk. There are Christmas decorations still around and mistletoe hanging in a doorway, on the drop chandelier, and other strategic places.

It turned out to be a comfortable and fun afternoon. We sat in front of a roaring fire, and he showed me pictures of his family. Both of his parents are dead, so most of the pictures are of him and his cousin Mark when they were young boys, also some of the dance orchestras he played with. The pictures of the young Paul are of a sad-eyed little boy. I gather he lost his parents at a very young age. Don't know how.

Before dinner he opened a bottle of wine and, though I paced myself, I felt a nice glow by the time dinner was served. The meal was ready except for finishing touches to an elegant fish dish. He is a darn good cook ... I'm impressed. More wine with dinner, which I sipped cautiously, I think, but confess I felt more relaxed than I have for a long time.

When I started to clear the table, he stopped me. His cleaning lady will be here tomorrow, I was told. He changed from background music to dance music and I didn't need to be coaxed. Oh, how I love to dance! After a few turns around the room, Paul stopped in the middle of a tune and just stood there with a grin on his face. I couldn't imagine what was happening until it dawned on me we were under the mistletoe.

I actually think I was blushing. What do I do now?

"Carmen, haven't you ever kissed a man you considered just a friend?

"Well, yes, of course. But since I've lived in California, it seems most of the men I've known misunderstand a friendly kiss and think it should lead to other things. Then when it doesn't, I'm a prude—or a tease."

"I like your honesty." He kissed me ... a nice, affectionate kiss, then continued to dance, stopping at intervals under the mistletoe. When he took me home, he asked if he'd lived up to his promise to behave. I had to admit he'd been a perfect host and gentleman.

It felt good to be kissed, especially in a lighthearted, non-demanding way. I've known since I first met Paul that sooner or later it would happen if we continued to see each other. Lately I've been feeling so alone and left out ... like I was a bystander and not a part of the life of my own generation. After all, what are a few kisses among friends? I've been worrying about leading him on. Shoot, he's a sophisticated doctor with lots of women friends; he certainly doesn't need me or my kisses.

I believe we are good friends. If it weren't for Harold, I'd probably be mad about him. I've cared about Harold since the first time we met, almost six years ago. I have to see this through to the end, no matter how long it takes.

I can't help but think how Harold must feel being away from home and family so long. He's the one who should complain. I know there are servicewomen where he is. I think about that a lot. I hope he's having a chance to dance and have some fun, and I hope someone nice is kissing him ... I guess! But I hope she's just nice and not drop-dead gorgeous.

1 JANUARY 1946
MAJOR H. L. HINER, USMC,
EIGHTH MILITARY POLICE BATTALION (PROV)
FLEET MARINE FORCE PACIFIC

c/o FLEET POST OFFICE,

SAN FRANCISCO, CALIFORNIA   BATEN KO

Evenin', Sparky Darlin',

Happy New Year and thanks so much for your packages. That's really a lovely gift and one which I can readily use. It is surely made of a fine piece of leather.

Believe I told you before that I've received both *War and Peace* and *Fountainhead*. Have started the latter and find it very interesting. Thanks a million for both of them.

Well, Carmen, I'm glad the Christmas rush is over so you can relax a bit. It's a wonder you weren't sick, with all the rest of the apartment sick and with the big workload you were carrying. Good woman!

I'm interested to know how your holiday (?) turned out. Were you able to get home for Xmas after all, or were you delayed? Surely hope you made it for Xmas, for I know what fun it would have been to get so much of your family together again.

What's the latest dope on Ham? Guess he didn't make it home for Xmas, did he?

Say, Carmen, do you remember Sergeant Major Rome. who was at Helen and Bob's apartment? Just received a letter and picture of himself and his cute bride. He's really a great guy! Surely isn't taking my boys long to tie those knots back there.

And so Doc is getting married, too? Guess you must have given him a real scalding to have driven him to such lengths.

How's my gal Alice taking Ev's absence? Be sure to give her my best. You can also tell her the party of the picture was a "good booze party" and that we'd be delighted to have you all on Okinawa! However, I do believe it will be better for me to do the traveling. I'll work on that idea.

Well, Sparky darlin', no news, and it's getting late. But—I did start the new year right! Love Hap

———— 🎵 ————

Dear Diary,

I've talked to Mr. Schwartzmann, and he will give me a week off to go home and see Ham if I do it before Irys leaves. Mr. "S" is really a peach of a guy, and I might add, a perfect gentleman. He's one of the few men I have encountered who is a boss or in a supervisory capacity who isn't on the make. He gave me a generous Christmas bonus and is helping me get train reservations. Guess I don't need to worry about being on a troop train this time.

I've been watching the mail, hoping for a letter from Harold. Haven't had one since his January 1st letter, which took longer to get here than his other letters have. I can't believe he wouldn't be writing, but nothing is getting through. Maybe I wished too successfully for him to have a nice girl kissing him. I'll learn.

Paul wants to drive me to the train station and pick me up when I return no matter what time of the day or night. I accepted his offer to take me to the station, but will catch a bus to work from the station on my return.

It's wonderful to be home. It's been six years since the family was together. I was at Utah State for my senior year when Ham left for what he thought would be a year with the army. Jackie and Granger are teenagers now, both Ham and Dick are married, and Dick and Fern have a four-year-old daughter, born while Dick was in England flying B-17s.

Mom and Dad are beside themselves with happiness. Mom's been cooking for days and Dad is walking on tiptoes ... that's what he does when he's happy. Life would be perfect if I'd heard from Harold before I left, but I didn't. I called my roommates to see if I'd received mail from him since I left, and I haven't. I can't understand it. I'm worried.

I visited Aunt Alt, Frank's mother. She's brokenhearted. She lost her husband years ago and her youngest son not too long after. Frank was all she had. When I think of all the mothers who have lost sons and the young women who have lost husbands in this war, I realize how lucky our family has been.

Of course, I have to take the 11:00 P.M. train from Lund to get back to L.A. It's quite a different trip than last time. There are a few soldiers on their way home, but mostly civilians. I'm in a sleeper car, and I turned in early hoping to get a good night's sleep. Actually, I had a hard time getting to sleep. I kept wondering if I would have mail from Harold when I got home and worried for fear I wouldn't. It just doesn't make sense, considering all the letters he's written when he was in combat, not to do so when hostilities are over. Of course, I don't know what his duties are. No doubt there are still some dangers out there.

I'm one of the first passengers off the train, and I regret having brought such a large bag, which I have to manage myself.

I was completely out of breath when I got to the street level. I put the bag down to get my bearings and, I'll be darned, Paul was coming toward me. I told him not to pick me up, but boy, am I glad to see him.

"Carmen, you shouldn't be carrying that heavy bag. I awakened early and realized I had time to pick you up before I had to be at the hospital. You're a sight for sore eyes." He got me to work on time and said he'd call after I had time to catch up on my rest.

That night I was too exhausted to eat anything. I checked the mail first thing. Nothing! Here it is almost the end of January, and I've had only one letter. Something's wrong. If I don't hear from Harold soon, I'm tempted to call his folks, though I feel sure they would let me know if there was good news ... or bad. It has to be the mail being improperly routed.

Irys's husband is home, and she's leaving at the end of this week. I'll have to do my job and help break in a replacement for her. That means longer hours and working on Saturdays. The hospital isn't very far from work, so Paul has been coming to the store after he's through for the day and taking me to dinner at a restaurant nearby when I have to work late. He's upset that I'm working such long hours, but it keeps my mind off thinking about Harold so much. Still no mail, and it's early February, a whole month since his last letter. When I get through with work, I don't want to go on a date. All I want to do is go home and fall in bed.

Things are finally easing up some at the store, and I'm getting home at a more reasonable hour. In fact, tonight I got home before any of my roommates. As usual, I stopped at the desk and picked up the mail. A quick look through it confirmed there was nothing important for me. I flopped on the couch and shook off my shoes. I felt like crying ... guess I'm just tired. The phone rang.

"Hello."

"Hello, Sparky? Hi, darlin'! It's me, Harold."

For a moment, I'm speechless. "Where are you?"

"I'm in San Francisco. I'll be in Los Angeles tomorrow. How about a date for dinner tomorrow night?"

If I live to be a hundred, I'll never know exactly what he said or what I said. I do know he will be coming by train, so I told him I'd meet him at Union Station. If Mr. S won't give me time off, I'll take it.

Before going to bed, I washed and pin-curled my hair and slept soundly in spite of my excitement and the steel bobby pins in my hair. I'm determined to look my best, and besides, the sound of his voice eased my worries of the past month. I put on my best suit and high heels and got to work early. Mr. S reacted as I was sure he would and said, "Leave whenever you please."

I arrived at the station ahead of schedule. I wanted to be sure I could find the right gate. It's been three long, agonizing years since we last saw each other. I'm alternately excited and then scared he'll be disappointed when he sees me; I positioned myself as close to the dividing rail as possible. When the passengers began to emerge from the tunnel, I scanned the oncoming faces for the one I've waited so long to see. At precisely the same instant, we saw each other. He was running, weaving in and out among the slow, casual travelers exiting the station. He hesitated only one second, realizing if he went through the exit gate, he would have to slow down and wait his turn. He was carrying a canvas overseas bag, but he charged full steam ahead, vaulted the waist-high rail separating us, dropped his bag, and did what any red-blooded marine would do in public ... only better than most.

I heard girls giggling, men cheering, and I didn't care. I never want this kiss to end. I heard someone say something about "coming up for air," and another voice remarking, "The marines have landed ... *Semper Fi.*"

Eventually, we did come up for air, but couldn't quit looking at each other for a long minute, then noticed a young marine standing by. He saluted, "Way to go, sir. *Semper Fi.*" Harold returned the salute, then reached for his bag, one arm still around my waist.

"I'll carry it for you, sir, and you won't have to let go a' her."

We walked to the surface transportation area, hanging on to each other for dear life, the sergeant walking behind us.

Harold with John Diehl the night he called Carmen to say he was home and would be in Los Angeles the next day.

CHAPTER 15

I'm in Love

I can't believe Harold and I are actually in the same country, much less the same city. He's sharing a room at the Ambassador with Robert, a fellow officer, who's much older than he and was on the same plane from Okinawa. Robert has access to a car, so they can stay in L.A. tonight instead of having to go straight to San Diego for an early-morning check-in.

Harold invited Alice and Robert to have dinner with us at the Ambassador. They entertained each other, which left us free to talk, hold hands, and sneak a few kisses. As well as I know Harold and as much as I care for him, our long separation has made me feel insecure . . . I guess. He's so much more sophisticated than the young man I knew in college, I wonder if I'm a disappointment to him. He doesn't act like it . . . but then, he's too much of a gentleman to be unkind.

When we got back to the apartment, Alice excused herself and went to bed. I wanted us to be alone, but Robert didn't seem to be in any hurry to leave. I freshened my makeup, and when I returned the two men were on the balcony in what looked like a serious conversation. I eavesdropped.

"Robert, you may as well turn in. I expect I'll be able to catch a streetcar to the hotel. If not, I'll walk. It's not like I haven't walked plenty of miles before."

"Well, Hap, I thought I should stick around. This is a really nice girl, you know. I'd hate to think you'd do anything you'd regret."

"My God, man, I don't need a chaperon! Don't you think I know what kind of a girl she is? Look ... I've just lived through five years wondering if I had a future. Tonight I believe I have and I wouldn't do anything to spoil it. I've waited a long time ... I can wait however long I have to. Go on, man ... I'll be back at the hotel in time to take off for Dago."

I returned to the bathroom and wiped off some of my lipstick. I've regained my confidence. He's going to get the kiss of his life. No more shrinking violet!

The next few hours were a bit of heaven on earth, a catching-up and renewal time.

"Darling, I know you have to go to work tomorrow. I don't want to keep you up too late. I'll report in tomorrow and pick up my orders, then, if you want me to, I'll come back here for a few days before I go to Phoenix on leave. Father wants me to join the agency; I have property in Phoenix, and when Jim gets home, all my family will be there. I have to decide the Marine Corps or the insurance business. I'll call you tomorrow evening."

The phone was ringing when I got home from work. Harold will be in L.A. early Sunday, and will stay until Tuesday afternoon. Happy days! I discussed it with Alice, Doris, and Ellen. We agreed he can sleep on our couch, because getting around on streetcars and buses wastes too much time.

Mr. Schwartzmann is allowing me to leave work early on the days Harold is in L.A., so HOORAY—more time together.

Two and a half glorious days. On his last evening, we were impatient until the others turned in and left us alone. Finally!

"Darling, I haven't had time to do any serious shopping, but there is something I've wanted to do for a long time." The words are barely spoken when I see he has his Sigma Nu pin in his hand.

"May I pin this where it belongs?"

I'll be darned, he didn't give it to *that girl* at Utah State, after all. Well, at least if he did, he got it back when they broke up.

"Sparky, while I'm gone, this will let the L.A. wolves know you're not available."

Paul Bradford called twice when I was out with Harold. I returned his calls, but he wasn't home. Tonight he showed up at the store and wants to take me to dinner.

"I tried to reach you to tell you Harold came home unexpectedly. That's why I was out the two nights you called."

"Are you engaged?"

"No, our time together was short. He's stationed at San Diego and will be on leave in Phoenix for a while, but will be back in L.A. soon. Its been a long separation."

"Surely, you can have dinner with me . . . we are friends, are we not?" After dinner, he reminded me again of my promise.

16 FEBRUARY 1946
PHOENIX, ARIZONA

Darling,

Saturday afternoon—and almost a week since I left you in Union Station. It has been a busy week, and I've really enjoyed every bit of it. But—I certainly have missed you. Hardly an hour has passed that I haven't thought of you and wished you were here. I hadn't expected to miss you quite so much after having spent only two and a half days with you, but I do!

The folks (Mother, Father, Harriet, and Burt) met me at the station, and we stopped at the Westward Ho Hotel for breakfast before coming home. "Home" turned out to be a very attractive one in a lovely district. I like it, the city, and the climate a great deal. As I believe I told you, Harriet and Burt are living with my parents until they can get their own house built. Their plans for their home were completed about three days ago, and their house should be delightful. Hope they can get it started soon.

The weather has really been beautiful, with brisk, clear nights (complete with moon, as you may have noticed) and clear, warm days. I've been yearning for a sunbath, but so far

I've been unable to sandwich one in. Bet I make it tomorrow, though.

P.S. 2/19 didn't.

Dear Diary,

Harold sent a lovely bouquet of twelve red roses for Valentine's Day. Guess he hasn't forgotten me.)

19 FEBRUARY 1946

Darling,

I am really conscience-stricken at not having sent a letter on its way before now. Father and Burt came early Saturday afternoon, interrupted my letter, and bundled the family off for a lovely sunset picnic in South Mountain Park. It was really beautiful, and I do wish you had been along. Then, Sunday, we took off bright and early for a truly beautiful trip down over the Apache Trail.

So, at long last, I am again seated before this letter and am determined to finish it before I go to town to lunch with Father. I received your sweet letter of the 16th yesterday, and it made me feel even worse at not having written.

Surely was glad to learn Leora's boy had arrived, and I'll bet Scott is truly the proud "poppa." Sorry to hear Alice is crippled up and hope she soon recovers—but I'm glad I left the Indian sign on you if it'll help to keep the L.A. wolves at bay.

Carmen, I surely will be glad when you can meet Harriet and Burt. They are truly a wonderful couple, and I know you'll just love them. I have always thought the world of Burt, but the better I get to know him, the more proud I am to have him for my brother-in-law.

Haven't received the modification of my orders as yet, Sparky, darling, but I'm quite certain I'll be sent to Dago (San Diego). Believe I'll have to report in there around the 13th or 14th, and I plan to spend two or three more days in L.A. en route to San Diego. So—I'll be seeing you around the 11th, I expect. I'll let you know as my plans become more definite.

Good-bye for now, honey, and it won't be so long before the next letter—I swear it. Please give my regards to the lucky gals who live with you and my love to Sister Alice. Love, Harold

Because Lyle Hiner had taken over the Arizona agency for the Mutual and United of Omaha Insurance Company while Harold was overseas, their home and the state of Arizona were new to him. Harold, however, had sent money home from overseas and had Lyle invest it in property on Bethany Home Road, next door to Harriet and Burt's property.

PHOENIX, ARIZONA
6 MARCH 1946

Dearest,

It's been too long since I left you. I opened my mail before going to bed, and what do you think I found? A wedding announcement from Elkins. He did marry Gladys Barron, after all.

I must tell you more about Bob and Gladys. They are the cutest couple. She seems just right for Bob; I know you'd love her. They arrived yesterday. They spent the evening with us, then today I took them all over the valley. They are going to live in a cabin about ten miles up Logan Canyon, and Bob will finish college and graduate—at long last. Lucky kids.

Well, darling, I had wonderful luck on my reservation. I leave here at 11:40 A.M. and arrive at Burbank at 12:03 P.M. on flight #9. So—we do get two days together. Honey, I do miss you. I miss you all the time, but I miss you most when I go to bed at night or after I awaken in the morning, for it's so quiet then. I wish you were here, darling, but I shall soon be there, and this time I won't have to waste all my time in trying to leave.

I'm leaving tomorrow for a two-day business trip to

Kingman with father. We'll get in Saturday night, Sunday I pack, and Monday I'll be seeing you.

We're off for the airport. Take care of yourself. Give my love to Alice and my best to the gals.

Good night, sweetheart, See you soon. Love, Harold

We've talked on the phone several times, but today I'll see him. I can't wait. I'm afraid I'm head over heels in love with him. I'll be at work when he arrives.

Midafternoon I looked up expecting to see a new customer at my window, and there he was, grinning from ear to ear. Mr. Schwartzmann told me to balance my cash and have Teresa take over for me. While I did that, I noticed he was talking to my favorite store salesman.

We had two perfect days together. Both mornings, when I left for work, he insisted on coming to the streetcar stop with me, because he says the passenger island is too exposed and is dangerous. He comes to the store and rides home with me after work to make sure I'm safe. I wonder how he thinks I've survived in this big city so far.

I believe he LOVES me!

Darn. He has to report in at San Diego tomorrow. Seems we're always saying good-bye. I wonder if that will ever change. My roommates are good sports, they leave us alone as much as possible. The instant their bedroom door closes, we're in our own wonderful world.

Harold has been unusually serious today. I think he has something on his mind. Finally we are alone, his arms are around me, and it hits me . . . this is the beginning of our future together. "Carmen, I love you with all my heart and have for a long time. I can't imagine a future without you in it." Like magic, he's holding an ivory and gold object, which I recognize as a Rhodes Jewelers ring case. "Will you marry me?"

My heart was pounding! "Yes, YES! I love you, my darling

wonderful man, and always will." Why am I crying, I wonder? I've never been this happy in all my life.

After he put the beautiful ring on my finger, he showed me its companion. "I want to put this ring on this same finger as soon as humanly possible." He took me in his arms and kissed me as I've never been kissed before.

Harold called from Camp Pendleton as soon as he was processed. "When can you come to L.A.?" I asked. "It seems more like weeks than days since I saw you. I miss you!"

"I miss you as well, darling. However ... I've talked to the base doctor about being circumcised—"

"Circumcised!!!"

"—and he says he can do it right away. The surgery is scheduled for this coming Thursday."

"Darling would—would you like me to come down there over the weekend? I can take a bus, and I'm sure I can get a hotel reservation in San Diego or Oceanside. I want to see you ... and hold your hand."

"I'll let you know, sweetheart. Pendleton is a big base and getting around it is difficult. I'd be worried about you. I'll see what I can work out." He decided I shouldn't come.

19 March 1946
Major H.L. Hiner, USMC
13-Qa-1 Camp Joseph H. Pendleton,
Oceanside, California

Good morning, sweetheart,

I love you so and miss you so. I wish I were to be seeing you today. I dreamed of you all night long—and it was a long night.

I had hoped to write you last night, but was so dopey it was impossible. I got up at about 2000 to go to the head and almost passed out before making the fifteen feet back to my bunk.

A couple of bright, pleasant young doctors performed the

operation yesterday at 1030, and a very neat job they did of it, too. I gave them your instructions—to be careful and not to dare damage the merchandise, and I believe they carried them out to the letter. The pain of the operation itself is negligible, but that "prepping" is the damnedest operation known to man or beast. Thought I'd go nuts before they finished shaving me. The only pain I've suffered was when the Novocain wore off and again at midnight when I lay for an hour feeling entirely too healthy, with an ice pack, which had become a bag of warm water. The mental pain in such a case is almost as bad as the physical, for one realizes that he is absolutely at the mercy of his reflexes, hardly dares to breathe, and just lies there wondering if the stitches will hold and what the ultimate damage will be. Finally, in desperation, I summoned courage to drag myself to the ward office to have my icepack refilled. Since then, darling, I have religiously "kept it on ice for you."

Have just returned from the morning's dressing and find that everything is perfect. Should be around in a minimum of time. Enough of the sordid details, but my usual lustiness, so evident already in this letter, should convince you that I really am in good shape.

What's the latest news from 401, darling? Who's helping you with the dishes, and are they as much fun as when we do them together? Are you catching up on your rest? You'd better be, for as soon as they unwind me here, I'm bound for L.A. on the double.

Hope Doris isn't having any trouble getting into the bathroom these mornings and that Alice is still managing to keep Dr. "Keta" at bay. Say, was Ellen serious about getting married? Poor guy!

Be very, very careful of my darling. More tomorrow. All my love, sweetheart, Harold

The last time Harold was here and slept on the couch, he got up at the crack of dawn to shower and shave before the rest of us were awake. Because he knew we were all aware he was here, he didn't lock the door to the bathroom.

Doris, who is blind as a bat without her glasses, got up early, forgot about him, didn't put her glasses on, and stumbled into the bathroom, nude as a jaybird. When the realization hit her, she ran back and threw herself on the bed, vowing never to get out of bed again as long as she lived. Later she regretted that, while he obviously saw her in the nude, she was too blind without her glasses to see him in the same state.

---

20 MARCH 1946
CAMP PENDLETON

Hello little sweetheart,

Surely is lonely lying here, looking out over these rain-swept hills, thinking of my sweet redhead. I miss you so, darling. More than you're missing me, I'm sure, for you have your work to keep your mind occupied. But I hope you're missing me like hell at night.

As for my physical condition, my progress continues excellent. Didn't sleep too well last night, however. Just too damned healthy for my own good. Of course, I guess it might be of some help if I didn't think of you 23½ hours a day.

Failed to tell you of my set-up here. I was placed by myself in a large, light, double room, with a bath which I share with a commander in the next room. As far as the conveniences are concerned, I'm entirely comfortable, and conditions would have been ideal for you to visit me here were the blamed camp not so extensive nor so far from Oceanside. Still believe it was wiser not to have you come, but I want so badly to see you, I'm almost sorry I was "wise."

Have a couple of damned nice corpsmen here who take care of me. One is a tall, humorous redhead who sticks his head in every hour or so to see if he can give me a shot of penicillin or something just for the hell of it. The other is a quiet, competent German by the name of Schroeder, who prepped me initially and who dresses my "wounds" daily. All in all, things are as pleasant as possible—considering I'm a hundred miles from you, darling.

Oh, sweetheart, I love you so! Nothing we don't share will

ever again seem very important. I can close my eyes and see you in so many moods—and all of them I love.

I read the *Black Rose* last night and enjoyed it thoroughly— can't say, however, that I think Mr. Ross, dear man, quite did the book justice. I was really biting my nails for fear Maryann would never reach London and that dear Wat would fall into the clutches of that horrible blonde.

Enough for now, darling. Hope I hear from you today. Love you, Harold

P.S. I just called up and learn I have two letters. Guess at least one is from you. Bringing them down right away. Thank you, darling. Love, H

21 March 1946
Camp Pendleton

Hello little sweetheart,

Both of the letters at my quarters yesterday were from you, and I loved them so. I had hardly dared hope for two so quickly. Darling, it was wonderful of you to drop me a note right after I left. Oh, I love you so very much!

Honey, as far as the invitation list from my folks is concerned, I put in a request for one last night.

Darling, at last I can tell you that you're not marrying such a common man as I had thought. The doctor says I'm one in a thousand. Small pride there is in it, though. Seems I'm allergic to merthiolate (more specifically—mercury), and as my pelvic region was liberally sprayed while prepping me, I now have a very annoying rash. In fact, it really is the most irritating thing of the whole operation, for, while I've had only a few moments of pain daily, this abominable (or should I say "abdominal") itching is continuous. One bright note, however, is that while sunbathing in the privacy of our back yard at home, I had so exposed myself that I had no more than a G-string of white skin left. And—the tanned skin is not sensitive at all, though acres were sprayed. Wish I'd had a 100% tan.

Happy day, dearest. I just called up the quarters and find

there's another letter up there from you. They're going to send the ambulance for it soon.

So your mother is already worrying and fretting about the wedding? I guess we actually did her no favor by telling her so far ahead. Golly, she must be a fine woman. I'm really anxious to meet her. I have always considered the "in-laws" one is to get to be of tremendous importance, and I know I'm going to love all of your family. I hope they just like me half as much as I know I shall them.

Oh, sweetheart, the more we're apart now, the more fully do I realize that any time not spent with you or directly for you is truly wasted! I love you so fully, so completely. There is only one compensation at being away from you at this particular time, and that is that to see you and be with you now would literally be more than flesh could bear. As I intimated before, darling, it matters not how sweet and lofty my thoughts when I'm with you, I'm yours completely, and my physical reaction to you is something over which I have no control. Not that I want to, for what could be more proper.

Dearest, dearest, I love you so completely in every way!

Good night, my love, soon I shall be with you again. Harold

I must keep my promise to Paul. He has been a good friend, and I want to tell him, in person, how much I appreciate his friendship. Also I promised David, the young amputee at the center, I would not forget him.

On the weekend, I caught the center bus at the usual place. I visited David first and found him much improved and actually excited about the new wheelchair, made especially for him. His eyes brightened when I walked in the room, and he said:

"I told them you wouldn't forget me."

Paul was in his office. He noticed the ring as soon as I walked through the door. He got up from his desk and walked toward me, took my hand, and looked at the ring.

"Thank you for coming, Carmen. Looks like congratulations are in order," His voice sounded choked. "I'll admit I'd hoped for a different ending to our friendship. Perhaps if we'd met when you first came to town, I might have had a better chance."

We had a long visit and said our good-byes as we had met— over a cup of coffee. "If you *ever* need a friend, call me . . . promise?" He held on to my hand awhile, then walked to the door with me.

Luckily, I caught the last center bus to Broadway. I noticed a middle-aged couple I thought were staring at me, so I smiled at them. They smiled, and the lady said, "We don't mean to be rude, but you look so happy."

"I am . . . I'm in love."

At the Broadway stop I felt like running down the street shouting: I'm in love, I'm in love . . . instead, I boarded the streetcar and whispered it under my breath on the way home.

Harold and Carmen at the Ambassador Hotel in Los Angeles, California:
"Yes, there is a Santa Claus."

Harold en route to Camp Pendleton, where he would be stationed.

CHAPTER 16

Home Again

Good Evening, Sweetheart,

I hope you don't feel so "let down" tonight as I do. It seems so terribly pointless to me to be down here while you're up there in L.A. However, I suppose you do need some sleep, so catch up on it in a hurry, for Saturday afternoon I'll be on my way again.

Darling, I found six letters from you when I got back here today—five from January and February. Yes, at long last, I did receive those pictures. The portrait of you is gorgeous!

Had a lot of other mail, honey, among which was reassuring word from Washington. One of my friends whom I had asked to keep an eye on the progress of my resignation tells me prior to 30 June the Corps is to release over 5,000 officers. And indications are plain here also that efforts are being made to release officers as quickly as possible. Apparently another cut in the MC budget is causing this activity—all of which makes things look even more favorable as far as we're concerned. Now I really expect good news within three weeks at the most.

Feel much better tonight (physically) than I've felt since the operation. Dr. Griggs took his last look at me today and says that long ere May 12th I'll be ready for full-time duty.

Guess I'll turn in early, darling. Wish I were there trying to keep you in my arms. One of these times, I won't let you go. Good night, my sweetheart. All my love, Harold

Dear Diary,

Looks like our timing is working out okay. It's risky, but we've set the wedding date for May 12, trusting Harold will be released from the Corps by then.

I've given notice at the store and will be going home in about three weeks. Busy weeks, because I want to buy my wedding and trousseau dresses from Robinsons here in L.A. Cedar City doesn't have much to offer, and gas is still rationed, so I know I can't plan on driving to Salt Lake to shop. Somehow, by hook or crook, I've got to get a shoe stamp ... I can't see wearing navy or black shoes with a white wedding dress

I'm so in love, and even though it has been only two weeks since we were together, it seems like a month. Thank goodness it's the weekend and I'll see him today.

I didn't meet him at the station, because he wasn't sure when he would arrive. Now he's here, I realize he's still not entirely himself. Poor darling, swears he's fine, but he certainly isn't walking as briskly as usual. One thing is sure he couldn't vault a waist-high railing today!

This being Saturday, all three of my roommates are home. In order to have a little privacy, Harold suggested we take a walk over to MacArthur Park and get some fresh air and exercise. Its a beautiful day. Spring is in the air already. If ever there was an outdoor man, it's Harold. He loves the wide-open spaces and every creature that walks, swims, or flies interests him.

I noticed he seemed a bit uncomfortable by the time we got to the park, so I suggested we sit on a bench. The lake and surrounding area was alive with ducks and other waterfowl. Soon it became obvious that this is the mating season, for they are cavorting on land and in the water, intent upon marathon romance. The males were persistent even when the females grew weary and noisily told them off. Birds overhead chirped nonstop and dive bombed each other, engaged in their own amorous pursuits.

Poor darling man staggered to his feet and suggested we go elsewhere. Elsewhere is in a grove of trees with a picnic table, meant, I'm sure, to be a haven for lovers wanting privacy and peace. It was not to be. Before long, more birds flew in and, on the ground, squirrels scurried in a courting frenzy equal to the antics of the ducks on the lake.

"Oh, my God, darling, let's get out of here. I can't stand any more of this. I'll bet even the damn earthworms are making love."

We returned to the apartment, took chairs out to the balcony, and talked over our wedding plans. First, there's the matter of a car for the honeymoon. It's almost impossible to buy a car, even a used one, unless you are on a waiting list. Fortunately, Harold's father has an "in" with some Phoenix dealerships, so he's put us on several lists, but so far nothing has become available.

There's no question where we will spend our honeymoon. At Zion Canyon, of course. Zion is one of Harold's and my favorite places. It takes only a little over an hour to get there from Cedar City. After a long, drawn-out reception, we don't want to face a drive of several hours' duration.

Mother has already arranged for the music, as she does for every wedding in town. At least that's all settled.

We still haven't arranged for someone to perform the ceremony. Harold isn't Mormon, but it never occurred to me until now that there might be a problem with that, but I don't know? President Sargent would be my choice. He's stake president now, but he used to be bishop of our ward, and I've known him as long as I can remember. Harold's going to be in Cedar on his way to Phoenix after he receives his release orders from the Corps. I'll wait until then, and we'll go together to talk to him. By darn, he better marry us, or we'll live in sin.

Harold's orders for release from the Corps haven't come through as yet. However, orders to take command of a troop train transporting soldiers to Camp Lejeune for release from the Marine Corps have. A friend of his at Pendleton is from that area and asked him to drive his car back to Pendleton, which Harold agreed to do.

"I'll enjoy driving across the country, darling, and you can bet I'll be in better shape by the time I get back. Next time you see me, I won't be such a wimp."

I think he's adorable!

5 APRIL 1946

Dearest,

Have tried on each of the past two days to get a letter off to you, but our trip so far has been so fast (and consequently so rough) that my attempts were total failures. In fact, if this doesn't get a little better, I'll junk this. Writing is entirely out of the question.

For a troop train, they've really been pushing us along. We'll hit Memphis this afternoon, and it is entirely possible that we'll get in late tomorrow. If not, early Sunday. Should be able to clear Lejeune Sunday night possibly, or early Monday morning.

I'm really missing you, sweetheart. I have so much time to sit here and think of you and lie here and think of you. I'm on fire to hit the other end of this run and turn around to come flashing back to you. Never again will I be so far from you.

Are you catching up on your sleep, darling? And are you getting your shopping done? Have you found any shoes yet?

Well, sweetheart, take good care of yourself, and I'll try to scribble you a line again tomorrow. We're coming into a station, and I want to get this out, so I'll secure for now.

I love you with all my heart, sweetheart, and I'll be back with you at the earliest possible moment.

All my love, Harold   P.S. On the list, Lt. McCarthy is "Robert C." and Lt. McKay is "Robert J."

5 APRIL 1946
EN ROUTE TO LEJEUNE

Evening Dearest,

At last I have the opportunity to get off a decent letter to you. I got off a positively stinking one at Pine Bluff today. It really is exasperating to be jolted continuously while trying to write.

At the present (7:10 P.M.) we are in the yard at Memphis. We were all set to shove off from here half an hour ago when they discovered a broken wheel on our baggage car. So—now we are stuck for a couple hours while they change wheels. Personally, I welcome a layover, as it gives me a chance to write to you.

Also have a little later dope on schedules. We're not due into Columbia, S.C. until around 8 or 9 o'clock tomorrow evening, which means we should hit Lejeune early Sunday. I hope to complete the turnover that day and be ready to shove off for home—and you—early Monday. In any case, I'll let you know.

I intimated to you in that horrible scribble this morning just how very much I am missing you. Sweetheart, since I first saw you on my return to the States, I've been missing you when we're apart. Each time, I've missed you more. Now it's just too damned much! I think of you continuously during the daytime, and last night, after being awakened four times by trainmen for one thing or another, I realized each time that I'd been dreaming of you. Then, before going to sleep again, I'd lie and think drowsily of you some more. Dearest, you are the one really important thing in the world for me. God, but I love you! This trip actually has many compensations. No, they are not really compensations—rather brighter aspects: (1) the time for our wedding draws nearer, (2) the time for my release draws nearer, I hope, and (3) this is the last time we'll have to be far apart. Oh, sweetheart, I'll be so happy when we can always be together; when I can always wake up and find you at my side!

Dearest, you won't forget to include Pres. and Mrs. E.G. Peterson as well as Dean and Mrs. Jack Croft, will you? Hope, as you may well imagine, that you have run into no hitches. Guess your mother is still worrying, isn't she? Bless her sweet heart! Gad, but I'll be glad to get back there and pick you up and go to meet your family.

Trip has been pretty decent so far. These boys irritate me at times, but most of them have been well behaved. I've shut those in my car up several times when they've become too noisy, but there's nothing I can do about the smell, with no bathing facilities available. Could be worse, though.

Goodnight, dearest, dearest sweetheart, I love you with every breath. Harold

Harold's main concern is that his job isn't done unless he arrives at destination with all the men he started with. Each stop, particularly in the South, brings out loads of girls who stand along the tracks, lean out of office and apartment windows, and call to the soldiers. Some of the men try to jump train for a *quickie.* So before and after each scheduled stop, Harold musters them for roll call to make sure none are missing. Not surprisingly, some slip through the net. When that happens, he puts on his shore patrol gear—belt and pistol, brassard and nightstick—squares his jaw, and goes after them. He reaches Lejeune with all present and accounted for.

7 APRIL 1946
CAMP LEJEUNE

Sweetheart,

Checked into here with my trainload about 8 o'clock this morning, and was I ever glad to get rid of them. I didn't have any trouble I couldn't handle, but I felt as if I'd been living in a pack of wild animals for five days. Honest, darling, they made more noise in every station we came to than a whole trainload of circus animals. Surely was great to shove them into barracks and come on over to the BOQ for a shower and a clean bunk.

I couldn't get my release today, since it is Sunday, but I don't believe it will take me more than a couple hours after 0800 in the morning to clear out, and before dark I shall have put many miles between me and the old Atlantic.

As soon as I got squared away here, I called to see about that car, and it has already been delivered to me. It is in excellent shape and should give me no trouble whatsoever. I have been checking routes tonight on a map which shows driving times. The times shown indicate a 70-75 hr. trip; however, I'm quite certain it won't take me that long. I hope to make San Diego by Friday night. At any rate, I shall be able to tell definitely within two or three days, and when I can, I'll send you a telegram.

Ran into five of my classmates here and have just returned from a very pleasant evening at the club. It was also a very sober one for me, as I intend to be in good shape for that long trek home.

Sweetheart, will you please add another to the list for announcements, the wife of one of my best friends in the service. I know her well, as she was with Don in Quantico when we were last stateside. Mrs. Donald Asbury, 1055 Granville, Grandeur Hotel, Chicago, Illinois. She is, incidentally, expecting twins. Miss you like everything and love you with all my heart!! Harold

APRIL 20, 1946
CEDAR CITY, UTAH

Dear Diary,

It's good to be home. Harold couldn't come with me, because of the trip to Lejeune. He wants to visit as soon as possible so he can meet the family and we can go to Parowan for our wedding license.

It's been six years since the entire family was together. Now Dick and Ham are married and Dick is a father, Jackie and Granger are in high school. Things are not back to normal in the country yet, and in some ways they never will be. A lot has happened to people we care about, but we must be grateful that most of our loved ones are safe. Aunt Alt's Frank is buried in the local cemetery (at least the air force believes the remains sent to her are his), and cousin Francis Betenson is home from a German prison camp. The Russians liberated him and other American prisoners. I feel blessed to have my brothers and the man I love safely home. I wasn't sure I'd ever see this day. But here I am ... preparing for the most important day of my life, surrounded by the people I love.

My sister, Jackie, will be my maid of honor; my two sisters-in-law, bridesmaids; and Dick's four-year-old, Ann, flower girl. My brothers Dick, Ham, and Granger will usher.

I'm grateful for my parents, who have never failed any of us. Our mother, Beth, is the most talented, unselfish woman I've ever known. Our gentle-natured, shy father is quietly strong, capable, and the only man on earth who could be married to Beth and hold his own. They are a perfect pair. They love us completely and mean it when they say, "Our children are the nicest, smartest, best-looking kids in town." That isn't true, but they believe it, so we try our best not to disappoint them.

Harold's in Pendleton, still awaiting his orders. He's worried they might not come in time for the wedding ... or when they do, if he'll be released from Pendleton or have to go to Pocatello, Idaho, which is where he lived when he entered service.

He's anxious to get back to Phoenix and look for an apartment for us. Even though the war is over, apartments are like everything else ... almost impossible to find. His folks say, if all else fails we can stay with them until we find something.

"NO WAY," he says, and I agree. If we have to pitch a tent, at least we'll be together and by ourselves.

22 APRIL 1946

Good evening, Sweetheart,

It surely was wonderful to hear your voice a little while ago and to find you were safely home. I suppose it's "real" silly of me, but all of a sudden I can't trust anyone but me to take care of you properly. I had been uneasy all afternoon wondering how your trip had been. Darling, you stay home and be careful until I can get there to take care of you.

I had an easy trip down. I went to sleep before we were five minutes out of Phoenix and didn't awaken until the stewardess fastened my safety belt over San Diego. We landed at 9:15 (PST) and I caught the 10 o'clock bus out for Oceanside. Slept all the way and arrived in camp before lunch. Great to be back—
—like hell!!!

I was overjoyed to learn that my orders had arrived. I know that their sending me to Pocatello is strictly a stupid oversight on their part, and it's inconvenient for me, but rather than get involved in red tape trying to correct them, I'll take off for Pocatello and let them release me from there. I am absolutely certain, darling, that I am being sent there for separation, and I expect to find my orders awaiting me when I arrive.

Since you may not remember my schedule for the next few days, it runs as follows: I stand detached here on the 26th. Then, If I rate two days' travel time, as I believe, from here to Poky, I'll be due to report there on 1 May. Expect to be there only a day or two, but I'll let you know just as soon as I get there.

Little sweetheart, I surely have missed you today, and I guess it will be worse each day of the nineteen days to come. Right now it seems pretty empty to remind myself this is the last time. I love you so very, very much, and I miss you so! Sweetheart, do be careful and take care of yourself. I'll be with you as soon as possible. I love you with all my being, darling, and I exist only for you. Goodnight, sweet Carmen. Hope your dreams will be as lovely as mine.

23 April 1946, San Diego

Evening, Darling,

I wonder what you're doing or have been doing tonight. It's almost 2300 here and 2400 there, so I hope you're in bed by now. But I hope you thought of me and missed me before you went to sleep, because, sweetheart, I'm really missing you. I have been sitting here thinking of you in so many different moods and attitudes and missing you more all the time. I love you so, darling! God, but I hate to be separated from you.

Surely seems a waste of time to me to spend two more days sitting around here, but I'm all checked out and ready to leave now. But—my orders say the 26th and I can't leave until then, so guess I'll have to grin and bear it.

Decided several days ago that I was getting too soft, so yesterday I started some easy workouts. Hated the idea of folding on the trail in Zion and having you carry me down the mountain.

I'll bet your mother is worrying more and more about the wedding, isn't she? Wish I were there, but—I wouldn't be helping her worry; I'd be around "bottlenecking" all your efforts, I'll wager! What do you think? It's late, so guess I'll secure. I love you with all my heart, sweetheart. Take real good care of my darling. All my love, Harold

———🎵———

Dear Diary,

My mother is worrying about the wedding cake. Sugar is still rationed, but the 2nd Ward Relief Society ladies *think* they can come up with enough stamps among them and, if so, will make the cake. It won't be a big, fancy one with a bride and groom on top, but rather decorated sheet cakes.

I've just learned we goofed and the date picked for the wedding turns out to be Mother's Day, so none of the churches in town will be available at the time set for the ceremony. The only other alternative is the L.D.S. Institute, which I believe will be large enough. It has a lovely chapel and only family, out-of-town guests, and close relatives, and friends will be invited to the wedding. It'll work . . . I hope!

Cedar is small, and almost everyone in town expects to be invited to the reception . . . the guest list for it has grown beyond belief and, with none of the churches available, I don't know where we can have it. Certainly our house is not large enough to accommodate such a large number.

Everyone in town is trying to help out, but when I think about all that has to be done, I wonder if we wouldn't be better off to elope. But then I think of my handsome sweetheart all decked out in his marine dress blues and I'm convinced that standing alongside him on that day will be worth all the fuss.

It's Sunday, and I'm going to spend the morning with my mother, who will be making her usual Sunday-morning rounds. Cedar City has three church wards. Sunday school in the morning lasts about two hours and usually is attended by the entire family. Evening church is more for the grownups. Our family belongs to the 2nd ward, but most Sundays mother has to go to all three because someone in each one needs her to accompany them on the piano. And, of course, now we have a small Catholic church in town, and they don't have any parishioners who can play the piano or the organ, so Beth stops there most Sundays, as well.

Today she's playing a processional at the Catholic church, for Lois Mumford to sing at the 1st ward, then a group of little kids who are in her singing class at the 3rd ward. She'll end up in our ward playing for Bert Carpenter to sing. Not only can I visit with her as we drive from one church to the other, but I'll see people I know at all four. Sure enough, I saw old friends, classmates, former students, and some of my favorite teachers.

We also saw Tony Lambert, the local policeman, a high school classmate of mine. (I had a huge crush on him.) He stopped us because, as usual, Mother is exceeding the speed limit.

"Now, Beth, you know you're going too fast! My gosh, Carmen, what are you doing here? ... you look terrific. I wish you could convince your mother to slow down. I'm going to have to give you another warning, Mrs. Leigh." He winked at me.

"Well make it fast, I have to get to all four services this morning." She handed the citation to me to put in the glove compartment. I'm surprised to find it stuffed full of citations. She assured Tony she would slow down. Then took off in a cloud of dust.

In spite of the delay, we made it to our own ward in time for Bert's song and to see lots of people I know. I was hoping I'd see President Sargent and perhaps have a chance to talk to him, but no such luck.

CHAPTER 17

On Cloud Nine

Carmen Dearest,

I don't know why I sometimes try to kid myself where you're concerned. Several times while you were in L.A., unexpected opportunities presented themselves for me to go to L.A. ahead of the time I'd planned to go. And several times I came up to the room and tried to talk myself into waiting until the time I'd planned to go (for one stupid reason or another). A couple of times I even undressed and lay down and then, all of a sudden, I'd be up dressing and practically on my way to L.A.

And so it was tonight. I reasoned very sanely at dinner that tomorrow night would be the proper time to call you, after I had later dope as to the time I might reasonably expect to get out of L.A. and, consequently, arrive in Pocatello. So I came up to the room, undressed, and slipped into my robe, preparatory to writing some letters, and lay down for a moment to think things over. The things I kept thinking over were you and you and *you*! Within five minutes, I got up, dressed, and went below to call you. God, Carmen, I love you and miss you so very much! The thought that I have eighteen more days to go is really hard to take. It is only the knowledge that after this period we'll always be together that makes this bearable at all. Honey, I do love you with all my heart!

I'm glad I changed my mind about going to Phoenix first. This way, I'll arrive in Pocatello a full four days ahead of the time originally planned. Then, if my orders are there, I'll have that much longer to look for apartments after leaving Poky, and if they're not there—I'll need the extra time in Pocatello. However, sweetheart, let's keep our fingers crossed.

Good night, sweet. It surely was wonderful to hear your voice, but it made me miss you even more. I love you, Carmen, darling. Take good care of my sweetheart. All my love, Harold

25 APRIL 1946

Dearest,

I've just been lying here trying to read a book on the economics of insurance, and I'm blamed if I could concentrate on it for longer than two minutes at a time. The first thing I'd know, my mind would be right with you in Cedar. Honestly, darling, if I can't concentrate on my work any better after we're married, we'll starve! I know, though, that if you were here, and I could touch you, I'd be able to relax and get something done.

Specifically, tonight I've been thinking about the way you and Leora took off for the coast to go to work, with no jobs and no place to stay. Sweetheart, I don't believe I ever told you just how much I admire you for that and for sticking at it the way you two did during those first discouraging months. I'm so damned glad to be marrying a woman with the fine, bright courage you possess; and I love you so for it. In fact, Carmen, I love everything I have ever known about you—your sweetness, gentleness, poise, intelligence, courage, tolerance, honesty. In short, I love you from the tips of the toes on those lovely, slim legs to the top of your lovely red head—and with all my heart! Oh, dearest, I know I don't rate a woman as wonderful as you, but so help me God, I'll love you enough to make up for most of my shortcomings.

Sweet, if this is more illegible than usual, it's probably because I'm writing in bed. As you've probably already noticed, I have an aversion to lounging around in clothes, or in pressed ones at any rate (perhaps because I've pressed so many). So I came up and stripped; found the room too cold for comfort; had already packed my robe and was too lazy to unpack it; and so, I crawled into bed. Need I say—"wish you were here!" When I finish this, I'll crawl out, take my exercises, and slip back in for a good night's sleep. I'm all packed, though I'd have plenty of time to pack in the morning, as I'll be leaving Oceanside on the 12:25 train.

I received your letter of the 23rd today, and the wedding plans do sound like fun. Do the folks know you are counting on them in time for dinner on the 11th? If not, I suggest you write Father, and I'm sure he'll make it. For some strange reason, you seem to have made a hit with him.

Getting sleepy, darling. Be good to my tall, slim redhead. All my love ever, Harold   P.S. I love you. H

————🪕————

Dear Diary,

Harold called from Pocatello to tell me he is now a civilian. He will remain in the Marine Reserves, but from now on he's primarily a businessman. Hooray!

He'll come to Cedar on his way to Phoenix. The visit will be short ... just long enough to meet the family, talk to President Sargent about performing the ceremony, and get our wedding license in Parowan. Aunt Alt has offered her car for the run to Parowan and will go with us for the fun of it. She is so lonesome and sad about Frank, but she doesn't let her grief spoil other people's happiness.

Harold made an immediate hit with all the family, especially Dick. Harold spent a day with him at the cattle ranch out south and Dick can't get over what an expert horseman he is. Not only that, but when they tangled with a rattlesnake, relaxing in the shade of a bush, Harold grabbed it by the tail and snapped its head off. Dick is a tough cookie, but he goes ape around anything that crawls or slithers.

We made an appointment with President Sargent at his home. I introduced Harold and nervously launched into the purpose of our visit. Before I could get the words out, he took the initiative.

"I hear you are planning a wedding. I assume you're here to ask me to perform the ceremony. If so, I would consider it an honor."

I almost fainted. "Uhh ... Harold is not Mormon, and he doesn't plan to convert."

"I've heard a great deal about you, Harold, and I know Carmen well. I'm sure you both have the maturity to make this most important decision of your lives. If you continue to live as you have, being self-reliant and of service to others, you will be blessed as you so richly deserve."

We had a pleasant visit. President Sargent asked us a few questions: How long have we known each other, what have I been doing the last three years since I left home, and what does Harold plan to do now that the war is over? I couldn't have imagined it would be this simple.

As usual, we had very little privacy with so many people around. However, soon we'll be in our own place, we hope. No roommates, no family. Just the two of us. I can't wait! I love him so much and live for the day we will never have to say good-bye.

Harold has to get back to Phoenix and start looking for an apartment for us. Time is really running out. Even so, he wants me to come to Phoenix before the wedding to see the property he owns, meet Burt and Harriet and Jack Ramsom, the contractor who is building their house. It would save money for both of us to have our homes under construction at the same time.

I've told Harold I'll come for a long weekend, so it's all settled. The truth is we're both lonesome for the other, so any excuse to be together will do.

Cedar has a small airport, and now the war is over we have a commuter plane that flies in from Salt Lake, then on to Las Vegas and Phoenix. I'm apprehensive about flying on that little plane. It's an old, single-engine model and looks like it's held together with spit and glue. Ham drove me to the airport, and when I expressed doubts about the plane, he reminded me a small plane can put down most any place it has to. Small consolation when we took off and it bounced down the runway like a rubber ball, then dipped and climbed with every gust of wind as we gained altitude.

"Please, God, get me there and back. Now that I'm the happiest girl in the whole world, don't let anything bad happen to me," I prayed.

Once airborne, I relaxed until we reached the Grand Canyon. The instant we flew over the rim, the plane caught a downdraft and scared me out of my wits. That portion of the trip was pure agony with the plane lurching up and down. I was afraid I wouldn't make it to Las Vegas, much less Phoenix.

I loved Phoenix immediately. I hadn't realized how beautiful Arizona is. I envisioned it as desert, like the pictures I've seen of the Sahara Desert. Instead, the state is extremely mountainous. The desert blooms with its own variety of exotic and tropical plants. I'll admit Harold and I have a difficult time looking at anyone or anything except each other. Burt and Harriet are great. Already they treat me like a sister. I'm so lucky.

Lyle and Irene are just as charming and friendly as I remembered them from our meeting in Salt Lake. I feel more than welcome in this family. Lyle told me today that after meeting me in Salt Lake when Harold was home from the Savo Sea operation, he had hoped things would work out for us.

My first night in town, Lyle and Irene took us to the elegant Arizona Club, located on the top floor of a very high building in downtown Phoenix. All the employees made a point of stopping by our table to greet Harold and tell him how happy they were he was home safe and sound.

The next day, we drove out to 1307 East Bethany Home Road, which will be our address when our house is built. It is outside the city limits, surrounded by citrus groves. Harold's lot is two and a half acres next to Harriet and Burt's property. On the way out there we passed a ranch—style home with a horse barn and a corral with cattle in it.

"Oh, darling, look at those big cows," I blurted out.

Without a word, Harold slammed on the brakes, backed up, and stopped.

"What's the matter . . . what's the matter?"

"Look again, Carmen."

"What for?"

"You're some kind of a rancher's daughter. Don't even know the difference between a cow and a bull."

"Oh, you! I wasn't REALLY looking. I know the difference."

All too soon, the visit was over. I had to get home, as there is still a lot to do for the wedding. However, we did meet with Jack Ramson, and he's great. We've decided to have him build our house. How can two people be so much in love? I'm the happiest girl in the whole world.

---

2 MAY 1946
PHOENIX, ARIZONA

Dearest,

I surely was sorry to have to ask you to take care of ordering your own bouquet. It was exceedingly stupid of me to fail to consider the problem involved there before. Honestly, darling, you'll never know how much I hated to ask you to take care of that in addition to everything else. Will you please forgive me? I lay here on the deck in the living room for almost two hours considering the problem from all angles before I finally decided to call you. I know it's far from good, but it seemed to be the most practical solution.

[In Irene's handwriting.] "Hello, honey, I just wanted to tell you how glad we are that Harold picked you for our new little girl. Irene H."

Mother just came by on her way to bed; told me to tell you she loved you, said she bet I wouldn't, and so took the sheet to tell you herself. Consider yourself told.

Carmen dearest, I was really surprised to find how hard Burt and Harriet have been looking for an apartment for us. They have actually looked at several and have many more contacts and leads. They were almost certain we were set for the one I mentioned to you. Too bad that fell through. It really would have been a good deal. I'll keep you well posted on all developments. I'm surely optimistic as to the outcome, for a friend of the kids called a couple hours ago with two new, interesting leads.

Well, sweetheart, I'm done for tonight. That bus ride was a little rugged, and I did the lawn after I got in. Not quite used to so much heat, and it really drained me. Then, too, it's after midnight and—I don't have you here to inspire me.

I love you, Carmen dearest, with all my heart. I'm missing you 'til it hurts and long to be with you so. Take care of my sweet redhead. All my love ever, Harold

I wish Harold wouldn't be so upset about the bridal bouquet. He didn't take into account that Cedar is such a small town and things don't work like they do in the big cities. He thought he could handle it from Phoenix by wire. Then when he called to our one and only florist, he didn't know what to ask for with no pictures to look at and choose from. It's no big deal. I don't mind picking it out myself. He's such a perfectionist.

At least some things are working out. We have someone to marry us, and that's the most important thing. Now if Harold can find an apartment, we can rent or buy a car for the honeymoon and, if we can find a place large enough for the reception, we'll be in business.

3 May 1946
Phoenix, Arizona

Dearest

I'm surely happy to be writing this to you tonight, sweetheart. For today Harriet and I found an apartment. Talk about luck—and a bit of something else! We'd exhausted all the hot leads their friends had uncovered for us (at least all those we could check out today) and had decided to "cold canvass" a bit. We stopped at one attractive apartment, got a flat "no" with no hope for anything in the near future. We started on when I noticed a nice-looking place across the street, and then Harriet recalled that she and Burt used to know a couple who had lived there. We went in, and I finally roused the landlady, who told me she had nothing and no likelihood of anything soon. She seemed almost ready to close the door on us when Harriet told her the only reason we had stopped was that they had known a couple there. The old gal's ears went up on that. She asked who? Harriet replied, "The Hintons," and the gates fell! She invited us in, told us all the latest on "the Hintons," looked us over carefully, and finally told me she would have an apartment within a week which we could have until October. I really snapped it up!

The dope on the apartment, in case you are interested (I am kidding) is: large, airy living room, fair-sized bedroom, bath and kitchen. It faces on a patio at the end of a court and is on the end, giving us windows on three sides. The living room is really quite attractive. It is about as long as the one in our home, or perhaps a trifle longer, but not quite so wide. The entrance is in the center, with a French door on each side and a window in the end. The furniture is adequate and decent, and all in all, the place is really quite attractive. The location also is desirable and the surroundings nice. It is located about a block off North Central and about four blocks north of the Westward Ho Hotel, which means it's only about a ten-minute walk to the office.

I've really been amazed since I've been here at the interest a couple of their friends have shown in getting an apartment located for us. They've certainly been more than ordinarily nice. Guess that's just the kind of friends Burt and Harriet have. And Burt and Harriet have offered us their car for our honeymoon. Surely think that's wonderful of them.

Well, sweet Carmen, guess I'd better secure on this, for it's doggone late. Thanks for the three letters I received from you today, dearest. I love you, darling, and miss you with all my heart. The time grows short, and I'm truly impatient to return to you. Good night, sweetheart.

All my love ever, Harold

I can't believe how well everything has worked out and just in time. Harold's letter telling me he's found an apartment and that we will have Burt's and Harriet's car for our honeymoon makes everything perfect. When I got home from Phoenix, I learned that Al and Rayma Cline, good friends of the folks, had offered their home for the reception. It is a large house, and the weather should be warm enough to use the patio for any overflow.

It's just a week until the wedding. Mother is still fussing

around. Every day she finds something more to do ... or worry about. There have been bridal showers for me, and the house is filled with gifts and letters of well wishes from friends and relatives.

Dad, with his usual shy ways, tries to keep out of the way. Today, however, he came up to my room and knocked on the door. It was a special treat to have a visit with him ... just the two of us. We sat on my bed and, typically, the first thing he asked me was if I needed more money. I assured him I didn't.

Then I asked him a question that has been on my mind. "Dad, does it bother you that I'm not marrying a Mormon?" After all, he is one of ten children in a family whose grandparents walked across the plains for the privilege of worshiping as they chose. He and two other brothers served on a mission for the church because they were called, and in his family, you didn't refuse.

He smiled at me. "Of course not, Carmen. It's all the same. In fact, I came up here to tell you how proud I am of you ... and have always been. I am also proud of the young man you have chosen for your husband. I've been bragging all over town about him."

Carmen and Harold in Phoenix, where he is on leave.
"Seeing my future home."

CHAPTER 18

End of the Rainbow

Dear Diary,

Only one more week until I will be Mrs. Harold Hiner.
When I look back on the last five years, I can't believe the long
road we've traveled to reach this destination. Harold's been all
over the Pacific, the Mediterranean, and even parts of Europe.
He's run into friends on the streets of New York, San Francisco,
Oahu, Casablanca, Taranto, Italy, New Zealand, and Sydney,
Australia ... in New Guinea ports, on the beaches of Iwo Jima
and Okinawa.

My journey, though less spectacular, was still a big step for
a small-town girl. The miracle is that through all those years, the
young man I couldn't forget from the moment I first saw him
has survived the biggest military conflict in history and returned
home loving me as I love him. Thank you, Lord!

---

4 MAY 1946
PHOENIX, ARIZONA

Sweetheart,

Only five more days until I head for you. Golly, golly, am I
missing you! I surely do love you, darling.

Burt and Harriet and I went for a long drive tonight just

219

looking at houses and yards, and we wished you could have been with us. In fact, though of course I miss you like the very devil, it has been Burt or Harriet who have mentioned several times in the last few days how nice it would be if you were with us. It won't be long now!

Carmen, dearest, how did you make out on your bouquet and those for the attendants? I still feel like a very stupid ass over this deal on the bride's bouquet. That's one thing I should have and wanted to take care of myself. Surely will have to go to make that up to you.

We went out to our property this evening and sprayed for a couple of hours. Trying to kill out that Johnson grass. We're going out early in the morning and should be through by around noon. After that, the whole family plans to drive to Globe. That's quite a lovely drive. We'll make it soon.

Well, Carmen *MY* very dearest, it's almost midnight again and I must be up early and off for Bethany Home Road on the mañana, so guess I'd better secure for now. I love you with all my heart, darling, and I'm really getting impatient to come to claim you. However, the time is truly short now, so I guess I'll be able to hold up. Good night my very dearest.

All my love ever, Harold

5 MAY 1946
PHOENIX, ARIZONA

Carmen Dearest,

Burt, Harriet, and I have just returned from a drive out past our land. It was really lovely out there tonight—so cool and quiet. Darling, I can hardly wait until I have you with me always. The more I'm around Harriet and Burt, the more I miss you.

Sweetheart, as I told you in my letter last night, I am now planning to drive up Friday, and Harriet will come with me. We'll leave here by 0400 and should arrive in Cedar at about 1530. You may be sure that once we get under way, I'll waste no time in getting to my sweet redhead. I surely do love you, darling.

This afternoon the whole family went up to Globe, and all the way, I'd keep glancing at my watch and thinking, "1415—by this time a week from today we'll be married," or "1630—by this time we'll be having the reception." Or else I would just be wondering where you were and what you were doing. Oh, Carmen, I miss you so! I'm not really certain I'll ever get any work done unless you're right at my elbow to keep me from wondering about you.

Well, here I am again as I've been every night since I've been home, with the house all quiet and everyone turned in. Burt just carried Harriet in to bed as she had gone to sleep on the couch while waiting for him to finish the paper. Now I do feel close to you—and yet miss you so. Only four more days apart, Carmen dearest, and then I'll be heading north to claim you and keep you forever.

We had good news from Lillian yesterday. She had heard definitely from Jim that he will be home next month. We're surely glad to learn that. Too bad my little brother won't be home in time for our wedding.

Well, my very dearest, I guess I'd better secure for it has been a long day, and I'm really ready for the sack. Goodnight, sweet Carmen. I love you with all my heart. All my love, Harold

Harold called after they got home from Globe, and I told him about the talk with my father and how pleased I am at his reaction when I asked him if he minded I was not marrying a Mormon. "He really has bragged all over town about you, darling."

We both got a chuckle over our parents. When I was in Phoenix, Harold and Burt teased Irene constantly, asking in my presence if she remembers how she cried in the night when the family left Kaw City, Oklahoma, and moved to Salt Lake City.

Lyle lost everything they had in the '30s market crash so, when he was offered a job selling insurance in Utah, he accepted. They were forced to sell everything they owned except their car. Lyle borrowed the money Harold had saved selling rosebushes and delivering papers to get the family to Utah.

Irene cried for nights, wailing, "Oh, Lyle, all the kids will grow up and marry Mormons."

However she felt then, and I can't blame her, I know she loves me, as does Lyle, and both are as happy as my parents that we are getting married. I didn't think the boys should tease her about it, but now I realize they tease her because they can always get a rise out of her. Actually, I believe she enjoys the attention. She is so relieved and happy to have Harold home, nothing bothers her.

That is the beauty of the happy days we are living through. Everybody loves everybody else and, in spite of differences that trouble some people, it's obvious to us we are meant for each other and our families are behind us one hundred percent.

6 MAY 1946
PHOENIX, ARIZONA

Dearest,

I received two letters from you today, and I surely was glad to hear from you. It seems ages since I talked to you the other night. And—it seems ages until Friday morning when I can head north for you. Oh, darling, only three more days until I'll be seeing you—never to be leaving you again.

Spent the afternoon today putting a high shine on my buttons, belt ornaments, and shoes. Surely want to look my best for the biggest moment (so far) in my life.

I surely hope you will like the apartment, darling, and I really believe you will. It'll be wonderful when we're moved in there with no one to bother us. That will be the sweetest life I can imagine, but I reckon we'll probably starve, for I know I'll not want to leave it long enough to go earn us a living. You'll have to throw me out.

Well, sweetheart, I'm really dying for sleep. I'm losing more sleep here than I do with you—and here I don't enjoy it. I'll try to make some of it back in the next three days so I'll be in decent shape when I get to Cedar. Good night my love. I love you so, Carmen. Ever yours, Harold

7 MAY 1946
PHOENIX, ARIZONA

Carmen Darling,

I'm so happy to be writing this to you, realizing that this is the last letter I'll be writing to you for a long, long time. After this there'll be no need to write, for I'll never be far from your side. Oh, sweetheart, I'll be so damned glad when 0400 Friday morning arrives and I can take off for Utah. Right at this point, Burt and Duke (the dog) are really going around and around. What a pair!

I wish it were possible to let you know more definitely if Burt can come with us, but he simply doesn't know yet. In any event, if you request their room for Friday night—and get it—Harriet can use it, and she thought that's what she should do anyway, rather than crowd your family. I'm so much at home there, I didn't even consider it.

I hope all continues to go well with the wedding plans, Carmen. I'm really all set on this end, naturally enough, having had almost nothing to do but anticipate. I'm really all set to start packing. Have kept myself from it, as I didn't want to have too great an interval of waiting after I'd started packing. Oh, golly! I'll be a wreck if I can't see you soon.

Still haven't made up much of that sleep, dearest, but I'll try to catch some in the next two days, starting with a little right now.

Good night, Carmen, my very dearest. I love you with all my heart forever and ever. Harold

MAY 10
CEDAR CITY, UTAH

Tomorrow we will be together. It's hard to believe we will no longer have to rely on letters to know what the other is doing, where they are, or more importantly if they are well and safe.

Harold called after supper to tell me he plans to arrive by 1600 (good thing I understand navy talk) ... That's 4:00 P.M.

Dinner for the two families will be Saturday night at the Escalante Hotel. Mother has now reached the point of panic. She really is well organized, but she thinks she isn't and goes into a state of shock every hour on the hour. About all there is left to do, as far as I can see, is to transport chairs from the church to the Clines' for the reception. I promise her Harold will help with that on Saturday.

"I'm not going to count on it," she says. "If he's half as moon-eyed as you are, he'll do nothing but get in the way." She hands me a list of things she wants me to do tomorrow morning.

"I think I can get everything on this list done, but I must be cleaned up and looking my best by 3:30 tomorrow afternoon. Harold will be here by 4 o'clock."

"Carmen, he'll not make it by then. It's at least a twelve-hour drive without counting gas and food stops. You mark my word, he'll be lucky to be here by 6:00."

"He'll be here by 4:00. He said he would ... and he will!"

I'm a wreck! Even though I've worked hard today, I can't get to sleep. I can't get my mind off my sweetheart. Every day of the last five years I've thought about him and worried about his safety. It's hard to comprehend. There is no real reason to worry anymore, and in two more days we'll be together for the rest of our lives. "I thank you, precious Lord. I promise I will be a good wife and I'll learn to cook as fast as I can."

Mother let me sleep until I awakened at almost 10:00 A.M. Friday morning. Bless her heart, she says she wants me to be well rested. I didn't tell her my sleep was fitful because I had weird dreams about being in a huge kitchen and not knowing what any of the appliances or utensils were for. When I ask what she wants me to do first, she says she is pretty well caught up and for me to relax and do what I need to do to get ready for Harold's arrival.

I am ready at 3:30. I keep looking at my watch, and precisely at 4:00 I hear a car stop out front. I take a quick look at myself in the mirror and open the door just in time to see Harold, the driver's car door still ajar, jump over the last three steps to the porch. I didn't know any two human beings could be this happy! It is a while before we come up for air, and I realize that both Harriet and Burt are in the car and remember my manners.

Harold is staying with us in Dick and Ham's room. After dinner he asks Beth what he can do to help her.

"Oh ... tomorrow, if you and Carmen have a little time to take some chairs from the church to the Clines', you can do that, though actually I'm pretty well caught up. You two enjoy yourselves and do as you please until after the rehearsal dinner tomorrow night. I insist Carmen get to bed early that night however, and ON SUNDAY YOU ARE NOT ALLOWED TO SEE HER UNTIL SHE WALKS DOWN THE AISLE.

"All of your family's reservations are at the Escalante Hotel. I leave it to you to see they are comfortable and let me know if they need anything."

CHAPTER 19

Wedding Bells

Dear Diary,

May 12th, our wedding day, dawns bright and beautiful. The weather is perfect. Harold is up early, and Beth gives him a hearty breakfast. Her usual bacon and eggs, fresh fruit, coffee, and scones ... made from the dough of her homemade bread, cut in strips, and deep-fried. With her home-canned peach preserves, it's a breakfast fit for a king ... or a marine. When he finishes, he leaves to join his family at the hotel and get ready for the wedding at 1:00 P.M. I'm allowed to sleep in, and when I finally arise, Beth wants to fix the same breakfast for me. I'm too excited to eat that much but can't resist a couple of scones.

The morning is mostly a blur, but with the help of my mother and Jackie, I manage to get ready for this unforgettable day. I look in the mirror and I'm pleased. I know I'm not a raving beauty, but happiness is a wonderful beauty treatment, and today I feel pretty.

I wait in the bride's room with my attendants, listening to the lovely music made even more familiar as I recognize mother's touch on the piano, playing for Bert Carpenter to sing "God Gave Me You" and "Dawning." Then "Oh Promise Me," played on the violin by Professor Halverson, and finally, the bass voice of Mr. Sandgren singing "Still As The Night." Dad is waiting outside the door, looking proud and standing on tiptoes as he always does when he's pleased.

When we enter the chapel, I see Harold, standing straight as an arrow in his dress blues, every button and uniform ornament polished to glistening perfection. His eyes are focused on the entrance, and the look that comes over his face when I appear speaks volumes and leaves me with no doubt that he loves me as much as I love him. I'm not aware of walking down the aisle. All the faces around us are blurred, except his and Burt's, his best man's. When I reach him he whispers: "I love you ... you are beautiful."

PRESIDENT SARGENT: "Friends: This is a very auspicious occasion. One that comes with a great deal of beauty and forward looking. On the outside we have a beautiful day—the sun is bright and cheerful—the trees and flowers are in full bloom. These young people who stand before you also have blossomed into full manhood and full womanhood. It is an inspiration I am sure, to all of us, and an occasion for great satisfaction when young people of maturity and experience meet and become companions for life. Indeed, the principle of marriage is a principle attributed among people by God himself.

Real success in life comes only in this relationship. Marriage holds the greatest place, the greatest happiness, the greatest opportunities of any relationship into which man may enter.

Marriage is the relationship upon which our civilization rests. Without the home, without the family unit, our society could not stand. And just as strong as our family units are, so is our society. And just as strong as our family units are, so are our state and national organizations strong or weak. So marriage holds not only opportunities, beauty, and happiness, but also holds great responsibility. As these young people take these vows, I believe they will accept the responsibilities of married life. And because of their strength as individuals, the strength of their bond of love, society will be deeply benefited. So it is an important occasion when two splendid people join hands in matrimony. Who gives the bride in marriage?"

MR. LEIGH: "I do."

PRESIDENT SARGENT: "Harold Lyle Hiner, do you take Carmen Leigh by the right hand in the covenant you now enter to become her companion—to love, honor, and cherish her as long as you both live, and you hereby promise, and this you do in the presence of God?

HAROLD: "I do."

PRESIDENT SARGENT: "Carmen Leigh, do you take Harold Lyle Hiner by the right hand in the covenant you now enter to become his companion and wife—to love, honor and cherish him as long as you both live, and you hereby promise, and this you do in the presence of God?"

CARMEN: "I do."

PRESIDENT SARGENT: (Now present rings. Take each other by the right hand.) "In the authority vested in me, I pronounce you, Harold Lyle Hiner and Carmen Leigh, husband and wife, legally and lawfully wedded for the period of your natural life. You may now kiss as husband and wife.

"I am sure each of you feel now as I do that in your heart there is a prayer and a wish for these young people; I ask you now to join me in expressing it: "Our Father who art in Heaven: We present ourselves before thee at this time in humility and gratitude. We are grateful for peace—we are grateful for life itself. We are grateful now for the lives of these splendid young people. We are especially indebted to thee, Heavenly Father, for the safe return into his home and family and to us of this young soldier friend. We realize he has been in many grave dangers, and because he has returned to us well and strong and uninjured, we desire to express our gratitude, and we do so humbly and sincerely at this time. We are grateful for him. We are grateful for his usefulness and for the qualities of manhood and honor that he personifies. We are grateful for his bride and wife—that she too has developed into worthy womanhood and she deserves thy blessings. We admire her because of her ability and the standards of womanhood she represents. And now, oh God, as they have come together in marriage, we pray that thy holy spirit will accompany them through life. Guard and protect them against evil of every kind and nature. And Heavenly Father, wilt thou bless their union that much good shall come because of their capacity, ability, and willingness to serve. Heavenly Father, grant unto them peace of mind that they might go forward now as husband and wife and enjoy their life together. And we thank thee and desire to express our appreciation for them and our thanks unto thee. We pray for these blessings and we ask them humbly in the name of Jesus Christ, Amen."

Now comes the challenge. I've been gone from Cedar for three years, and I'm afraid I'll not remember people's names as I should. Jackie will be next to me in the receiving line so she can coach me. I swear whenever I see a pregnant young woman in the line, I know she's going to turn out to be a cousin. Harold's teasing me about the fertility level of the family. I remind him they didn't get that way all by themselves.

The reception is beautiful. Mother and Rayma have done a good job and we're enjoying it, but it's going on for a long time and there seems to be no let-up in the line. I'll admit we're both anxious to get on the road for Zion.

Dad just came by and offered to bring us something to drink. The receiving line is too solid for us to take a break and we're both dry as a bone. This being a Mormon community, no alcohol is being served, so I opt for punch and Harold chooses water. When we begin to think Dad's forgotten us, he returns. Harold takes one sip, then his eyes light up and he takes a healthy gulp.

"I say, Carmen, your dad is all right."

"Well, of course he is. Are you just finding that out?"

When there was a little break in the line, Harold whispered in my ear. "Your dad brought me a Scotch and water."

Dad's not an experienced bartender, but you can bet that drink is a lifesaver. Harold's wearing his dress uniform made of heavy wool, and the metal buttons and ornaments alone weigh a ton. Hardly the best attire for a warm summer day. He looks like the cat that swallowed the canary.

We are both getting restless and weary from standing so long. The crowd is dwindling down to stragglers, and in ten minutes it will be time to end the reception. We are relieved when Beth tells us we can leave whenever there is no one in the line.

"If people come after that," she says, "it's just too bad."

Right on the dot of five P.M. we go upstairs, change clothes, and take off. In just a little over an hour we are in our beloved Zion Canyon, checking into the honeymoon cottage.

We are alone ... no more roommates and no more family. After five long years we are together ... in heaven!!

It's late the next morning when we get up and around. We're both hungry, having eaten little the day of the wedding. When we open the door, we're greeted by a bevy of the park's summer employees ... waitresses, cabin girls, bellhops, and at least one bus driver. All high school and college kids from Cedar City. Kids I recognize from my classes when I taught high school there. They're sitting on the porch chairs, steps, and railing, giggling and giving us THE LOOK.

"Hi, Miss Leigh."

For the entire week of our stay in Zion, there is a contingent on our porch every morning. Of course, the girls whose job it is to clean our cabin are expected to be here. However, news travels fast and before we leave, I see most of the students I taught during my two years at Cedar High. After the shock of seeing them, I don't mind. I know them well and I know what's on their minds.

It's obvious that Harold's the main attraction for the girls, and soon he's joking with them and they're loving every minute of it. The day we hike up the East Rim Trail, it is so hot he wears his marine camouflage suit and the girls all but swoon when they see him.

When we get back from the hike, thirsty and hungry, we go to our favorite restaurant in Panguitch for breakfast. All the way down the trail, we talk about how good a cold beer will taste. It is Sunday and, dumb me, I forgot that no place in Utah would be selling beer on Sunday. My husband forgave me.

The last morning there, I'm surprised to see Clyde Parry in the group. He's standing away from the others, leaning against a tall pine tree. We stop and I introduce him to Harold.

"I heard you were here and wanted to stop by and tell you I will graduate from the University of Utah next spring in radio communications. Miss Leigh is the teacher who got me interested in that field," he explains to Harold. "Most of us senior guys had a case on her. You're a lucky man, sir."

   We both congratulate him, and I can't resist giving him a hug. It feels good to know I had some impact as a teacher.

   Next morning we leave for Phoenix to begin our life together. I am in love with the most wonderful man on this earth and I will thank God, every day of my life, for bringing him safely home to me.

Epilogue

The war officially ended over five months ago, September 1945, but it didn't feel like it to me until Harold came home and the man I loved took me in his arms. Within three months, we married. Now a civilian, a businessman in Phoenix, Arizona, his destiny was no longer in the hands of the U.S. Marine Corps.

We started construction on a fabulous ranch-style house on the two and a half acres his wartime salary had purchased and began making new friends.

Though the fate of many Americans was still in question and some of them were people we knew and cared about, for a while it seemed as though the war was truly over. Until one day I perused an issue of *Life* magazine and realized that for many, the war would never be over. Pictured were a man and woman in the living room of their farm home somewhere in the Midwest. Six flag-draped caskets filled the small room, and the pain on their faces was beyond description. Though they were strangers, I knew the picture would haunt me for the rest of my life.

Dick and Ham were home, and Cousin Frank was buried in the local cemetery. Another cousin, Francis Betenson, who had been missing since March 4, 1944, had finally been liberated. His was one of the sixteen B-17 bombers and twenty-six fighter planes shot down by the Luftwaffe that day. Brother Dick had flown the same mission and barely managed to bring his crippled B-17, Ice Cold Katy #11, back to home base. Until the war ended, it was not known if Francis was alive or dead.

For fourteen months, Francis had been held captive in a German prisoner-of-war camp. The small stove in each room provided little heat in the damp Baltic cold. By the rules of the Geneva Convention, officers could not be made to perform manual labor, so the prisoners fought boredom as well as the cold.

To pass the time, prisoners gave classes on their various fields of expertise. Francis, for example, taught accounting. They staged plays, and the camp had a good jazz band, which used instruments provided by the Swedish Red Cross. Even the Germans liked to attend the band's performances.

The spring of 1945 brought not only warmer weather but the hope of liberation, as Allied armies began their drive into the German heartland.

In May 1945, the Russians arrived. The liberators spent most of their time plundering the German countryside and little time helping the prisoners.

On May 13, Second Lt. Francis Betenson, weighing 134 pounds instead of his normal 165, boarded a B-17 for the flight to a Returning Allied Military Personnel camp near Le Havre, France. The camp was called Camp Lucky Strike. On January 30, 1946, he returned to Cedar City, Utah.

Two first cousins and some close friends were still missing and unaccounted for. In the ensuing months, the fate of two more of them was resolved.

Karl Burgess, the young man who lived with us after his father died and his mother took the younger children and left town, was freed from a remote German camp. We thought of Karl as a brother, and the whole family rejoiced to have him home. He made arrangements to enter college to pursue his dream of becoming a lawyer like his late father.

February 9, 1948, we had our first child, a daughter Christine. Our happiness knew no bounds. To us she was a miracle and the most beautiful baby ever born. Two days after we brought her home from the hospital, I had a call from my mother in Utah.

"You'll never guess who came to our door today," were her first words. Art Culver, the young man who took his cadet training in Cedar City when I taught high school there, had appeared unannounced. He was emaciated, with almost no hair on his head, and had been in an American veteran's hospital for most of the last year. Art had been a prisoner of the Japanese from the fall of 1943 until a year after the end of the war when he was found and brought home. When he was released from the veteran's hospital, he went to the Westmoreland apartment in Los Angeles where we had seen each other the night before he was sent to the Pacific. It was five years later, and the tenants now knew nothing of a Carmen Leigh.

Art came to Cedar City hoping to find out where I was.

Knowing there were lots of Leighs in town, and because he couldn't remember Dad's first name or the name of the street where we lived, he couldn't telephone, but believed once he was in town he could find our house.

Beth invited him in, gave him a hearty lunch, and they had a nice visit. She told me I was married and had a baby girl. She gave him our address and telephone number, but doubted he would call.

I was happy to learn that Art was home and should recover from his ordeal. I hoped someday he would find the happiness Harold and I found and that all those others out there still missing in action, whoever they may be, would be found before it was too late.

The fate of two other cousins and several friends we'd known before and during the war remain unknown.

The war years were unforgettable. I will never forget the people who shared that period of my life. The young women who were my roommates and friends will be important to me as long as I live. I plan to stay in touch with them.

Old Doc is now married. It's hard to believe that at age forty-two he would succumb to matrimony. My guess is that with the war over, he saw what he called his "harem" diminishing. He was a challenge at times, but at other times entertaining and a source of help and protection when we needed him.

I miss seeing some of the patients and staff at the Rehab Center, especially David and Dr. Paul Bradford, who was a good friend and a gentleman. I worry about David. He is young, and I know living with two artificial legs will be difficult for him.

The day before our wedding I received a congratulatory

telegram from Paul which also said: "If you *ever* need a friend, just pick up the phone and give me a call." During the next two years, he called Irys periodically to check on me.

The center was closed in 1948. Paul married his office nurse and went into private practice. When I heard he was married, I sent him a telegram with the same message he sent to me in 1946.

In 1948 *The Complete History of World War II* was published. It was written by Francis Trevelyan Miller Litt.D, LLD., with a board of 200 historical and military authorities from thirty nations, including Germany and Japan. In the late months of 1945-46, it was discovered that Japan had an army of 7,000,000 men, nearly double the highest estimate, of which 3,000,000 were on the home island and more were being withdrawn from the Continent.

Japan also had 6,000 to 9,000 planes hoarded to be launched against an invasion, which explained the lack of opposition to the Allied bombers and warships during pre-invasion. The Japanese planned to hurl these planes in suicide attacks (kamikaze) against the troopships and covering vessels. In addition, mines had been laid in the waters completely ringing Japan. They were in a position to inflict so much damage that the invasion troops (mostly American marines) could not cope with the island's defenses and would be slaughtered at the water's edge.

Japan had been practicing the worst kinds of torture and deprivation on its prisoners, even to the extent of cannibalism, by tying captured pilots to a stake, and carving off slices of their buttocks for cooking and eating.

According to *U.S. News and World Report* some 100,000 Allied prisoners of war in Japan had an even greater stake in the dropping of the bomb. Under orders from Tokyo, the moment the invasion of the Japanese Home Islands began, all POWs were to be beheaded, stabbed, or shot en masse, and at certain camps, American prisoners had been kept busy in recent days digging their own graves.

Had the atomic bomb not been completed at this time, it is estimated it would have taken, at the least, another year and a possible loss of a million or more men to end World War II.

Harold lived up to the saying "Once a marine, always a marine." His admiration and devotion to the Corps never waned. He remained in the reserve until eligible for retirement. In the intervening years, he conducted the Veterans Training Unit program for reservists in Tucson, Arizona, and achieved the rank of full colonel.

Carmen reunited with her best friends from Cedar City after the war. Top row, from left, Eloise (Lunt) Wayment, Leora (Petty) George, Lucille (Macfarlane) Crockett, and Carmen. Husbands, bottom row, from left, Elvin Wayment, Scott George, Vern Crockett, and Harold. The men all fought in World War II.

$\mathcal{B}ibliography$

BOOKS

Henri, Raymond. *Iwo Jima: Springboard to Final Victory*. New York: U.S. Camera Publishing Corp., 1945.

Miller, Francis Trevelyan. *The Complete History of World War II*. Chicago: Progress Research Corp., 1948.

Morris, Frank D. *"Pick Out the Biggest": Mike Moran and the Men of the Boise*. Boston: Houghton Mifflin, 1943.

NEWSPAPERS

The Arizona Daily Star.
Arizona Republic.
The Honolulu Advertiser.
San Francisco Examiner.
Stars and Stripes.

MAGAZINES

Life, July 11, 1943.
The Scholastic, November 12, 1942.
Time, November 30, 1942.

PERSONAL COLLECTION

Boise reunion publications, outlining the ship's World War II history.

Harrelson, Col. Jay B. "Bataan Death March," address.

Hiner, Harold, address to shipmates of the *Boise* at the 1973 *Boise* reunion.

———, audiotapes of conversations with his son.

Leigh, Henry H., personal memoirs.

U.S. State Department to the White House and the navy, official bulletins and news releases regarding the Savo Sea campaign and the opening of the second front in the Mediterranean.

Unknown reporter on the *Boise*, "Sicilian Invasion." Appeared in "Press News for all U.S. Ships and Stations," courtesy the UP Association.